# I AM
# DIVINE INNOCENCE

This work is entrusted to the patronage of St Joseph,
Head of the Holy Family and
Patron of the Universal Church

# I AM
# DIVINE INNOCENCE

*(words of Jesus to Patricia, 5 August 2017)*

Dudley Plunkett

Matador
9 Priory Business Park,
Wistow Road, Kibworth Beauchamp,
Leicestershire. LE8 0RX
Tel: 0116 279 2299
Email: books@troubador.co.uk
Web: www.troubador.co.uk/matador
Twitter: @matadorbooks

ISBN 978 1789015 898

British Library Cataloguing in Publication Data.
A catalogue record for this book is available from the British Library.

Printed and bound by CPI Group (UK) Ltd, Croydon, CR0 4YY
Typeset in 12pt Minion Pro by Troubador Publishing Ltd, Leicester, UK

Matador is an imprint of Troubador Publishing Ltd

# Contents

# Introduction

This book concerns the private revelations of Christ's Divine Innocence given to Patricia de Menezes since 1984 and their implications for the Catholic Church and for secular society. Through detailed messages Our Lord reveals that he wishes all people to recognise God's Divine Innocence made visible in his person when he was born into the Holy Family in Bethlehem. In his Divine Innocence, Jesus was crucified on the Cross and won for all humanity a victory over sin and death. At the Resurrection, Divine Innocence rose triumphant from the dead. But Jesus has also come into the world to return to us our innocence, which has been crucified either by our own sins or the sins of others, so that his Divine Innocence can be triumphant in our wounded or crucified innocence.

The book is in three parts. In the first part, *How the Events Unfolded*, there is an account of Patricia's life, both before and after the beginning of the revelations and teaching from heaven, which are still continuing at the time of writing. It was thought important to inform readers about the life of the person witnessing to the revelations, a mother, grandmother and jewellery designer, fashion designer and craftswoman, who was received into the Church as an adult in 1967 but was largely ignorant of the Catholic faith when her mystical experiences began. Our Lord and Our Lady began to teach Patricia through the experiences of her past life and her knowledge as a jewellery and fashion designer, speaking to her of '*a new robe of innocence*' and the purification of the soul, like gold purified by fire.

The second part, *Spiritual Insights of the Way of Divine Innocence*, summarises the content of the private revelations and how these were communicated in messages and visions from Jesus and his mother, Mary, showing that the divine Order of the Holy Family is the original Catholic Christian home offered to all humanity, a real family home on earth and a living reality, a school for holiness, a refuge for believers and a help towards their salvation. The messages also contain a request to the Church to recognise children who are innocent victims of abortion as companion martyrs of the Holy Innocents of Bethlehem, and therefore saints in heaven.

The third part, *Divine Innocence in the Church and Society*, proposes a justification for this divine grace to be taken seriously into account by the Church authorities and by society at large if there is to be any hope for peace and holiness to reign in families and between nations. When Patricia asked Our Lord what was the essential purpose of the Order of the Holy Family, he said: "*In preparation for My second coming*", indicating how he was offering a special grace and enlightenment so that he will indeed find faith on earth when he comes again. The messages relating to the Lord's request to the Church to claim the victims of abortion as martyrs are especially important since this multitude of *new Holy Innocents,* when raised to the altar of the Catholic Church and proclaimed saints, will become an army of witnesses and intercessors who, through their prayers, can speak in every language and in every nation, calling all to repentance for their deaths and seeking God's mercy and forgiveness.

## What is a Witness?

The word 'witness' is an important one in this book, and indeed in Catholic life since the original preaching of the Apostles, so it is worth pausing for a moment to consider its possible meanings. Essentially, witness is evidence given about a personal experience, something seen or heard. In this case there is first of all the inner credibility of the messages and how they stand up. The messages themselves provide the greatest witness to their own authenticity, since their coherence, fidelity to Church doctrine and depth all testify to their divine origin.

There is also the credibility of 'the witness', that is the person giving this testimony, in this case Patricia, the instrument of the divine revelations. Based upon her witness, this book reports what she affirms without repeatedly reminding the reader that she is not laying claim to publicly established facts but witnessing to what she has heard and seen. Patricia is taken as a witness not just of the messages but of the experience of receiving them, as will be seen in chapter 3 on the impact they had on her spiritual and prayer life. This personal testimony makes the text live not only by what the heavenly figures say but through its current impact and relevance.

Patricia herself had no Catholic background at the time when these inspirations commenced, since her only connection with the Church was through her Goan Catholic husband, while she herself came from a Salvation Army family. Neither did she have any significant cultural background beyond the jewellery design qualifications she had acquired. Another factor is that Patricia suffers from dyslexia, which limited her reading and caused her considerable difficulties in the theological studies that she eventually undertook in the 1990s, long after the messages had begun.

As far as the crucial witness of Patricia is concerned, the inspiration manifests itself in various ways. It draws upon the understanding of the person concerned and their experience over time. God works with the personality and life experiences of the instrument, in this case of Protestant background, a sinner called to conversion. The one chosen had little knowledge of the Catholic faith and even a certain historical suspicion and fear of the Catholic Church and its beliefs. Patricia was very much in need of enlightenment and instruction.

*In Patricia's own words.*[2] The experience is tactile, audible, and infused knowledge depending on what is being taught. For example, I was shown

---

2    It is evident that Patricia's own words of testimony are essential to fully convey the teaching in the Divine Innocence messages. In *Part Two* this involves substantial quotation interspersed with essential introduction and commentary. To make it clear when direct speech is used all quotations are indented.

the Apostles walking with Our Lord along a dusty road. It is as if I was there with them and I could see the dust rising as they walk along. Our Lord's suffering at the Crucifixion is vivid and real. I heard the cries of the Child Jesus clearly, and I felt the softness of his hair. Our Lady was shown in a magnificent procession with angels and saints. At other times I saw her suffering beneath the Cross.

Later, as I became attuned to the way I was being enlightened, a kind of shorthand is employed. Some visions do not need to be repeated, just a glance towards earlier instruction is enough accompanied by new insights. Scripture tells us that such gifts are affected by the imperfect state of the instrument. As a personal example, when I was preparing a catechism class for a pupil Our Lord said the person could not come that day. I did not trust the inspiration and continued the preparations. But the person did not arrive. I realised I needed to learn discernment and trust.

A person given these graces needs the Sacraments, advice from priests, spiritual friends with sound reason and good judgement, and time for discernment and prayer. All this Our Lord arranged for us. We were also careful to seek out the help of theologians in good standing in the Church regarding the content of the Divine Innocence inspiration. (23/3/2017)

Pope Paul VI affirmed that for the announcing of the Gospel the world needs witnesses rather than teachers (*Evangelii Nuntiandi*, para. 41). An implication of this view is that direct experience is more compelling than descriptions and arguments, that truth is more important than any speculative comment, and that sincere love is more relevant than intellectual interest or exploration. The mere existence of a witness does not, of course, ensure proof but it increases the plausibility and probability of right discernment of events including, most importantly, whether the person's life has changed for the better and whether anything is being said that is contrary to Scripture or to Catholic faith and morals.

There is the witness of the Holy Family itself which, by its faithfulness, the clear roles of each of its members, its protection and its nurturing of the Infant Jesus, testifies against sexual irresponsibility, promiscuity, confusion of genders, child abuse or neglect, and the killing of the unborn. The children killed by abortion are being put forward as chosen instruments by God to be universal martyr witnesses with their lives to the Truth who is Christ, and to the Gospel and teachings of the Catholic Church.

The author of this book is another kind of witness. If Patricia is in a sense an interested party with regard to her private revelation, then one who seeks to chronicle the phenomenon aspires to be disinterested, that is a witness as an outsider to the events and inspiration recorded in this work but seeking to capture the message confided to Patricia for a general audience.

I have never doubted the veracity of the witness given by Patricia and have been struck by her humility, humour and confidence in knowing what she wants to say; I have seen it as my responsibility to be positively critical of the inspiration, testing the spirit for integrity, coherence and fruit. What I found has impacted me strongly, and this is part of what I have to communicate. It was only when I became involved with preparing this work that I found myself propelled towards making my own commitment to the Way of Divine Innocence. Why did I delay so long? I could say that I was so closely associated with the Medjugorje apparitions of the Virgin Mary, about which I have written a book and more than a hundred articles, that I felt it inappropriate to be divided in my attention.

The insight that has come to me in the recent past is that the Way of Divine Innocence is fully compatible with the guidance given by Our Lady in numerous apparitions: the place of prayer, the Mass, the Rosary, the Bible and the Sacraments in coming to personal holiness and salvation. The fact is that, although I had read many of the messages Patricia received, I had not adequately grasped their import, and it is only with the effort to summarise them that I have come to a fuller appreciation of their coherence. I had seen Divine Innocence as simply another option for the spiritual life. I did not imagine that by becoming a member of the Holy Family, in the intimate way Our Lord's invitation put forward, I would gain further heavenly guidance. In fact, it is much more plausible that the Way of Divine Innocence can only truly be explored by living it.

Now, more than thirty years after the first messages received by Patricia, her personal witness is enhanced by a 'cloud of witnesses' (Hebrews 12:1) who have found their faith stimulated or renewed by the Way of Divine

Innocence and who can attest to the truth and value of her inspiration, as we shall see in *Part Two*. It will be for each reader to judge how to respond to the messages. They are summarised here with a minimum of commentary, but they will be authenticated by how far the reader, in meditating upon them, finds a deeper unity with the Holy Family centred upon the Divine Innocence of Jesus.

# PART ONE

*How The Events Unfolded*

# Chapter One

∞

# Patricia's Life
# before the Messages

Patricia never expected to hear the voices of Jesus and Our Lady speaking to her, and certainly not to be entrusted by Jesus with the task of both establishing a community and testifying that the children who are victims of abortion have a mission in the Catholic Church. At present the Divine Innocence Community has two foundation houses on the former site of the Catholic Manor House Convent School in Surbiton, Surrey. It is there that I visited Patricia in November 2016 and agreed to work with her to record her witness account of her private revelation and all that has developed from it.[2]

This was not my first contact with Patricia. I had first heard about her in 1985, soon after her mission began, and

---

2    The quotations in Patricia's own words in Part 1 were recorded in a
     series of interviews with the author between November 2016 and May
     2017. In Parts 2 and 3, quotations taken from other documents are given
     with their original dates.

since that time remained in touch, reading the materials that the Community of the Divine Innocence provided, and following its progress. In the meantime, I published a book, *Heaven Wants to be Heard*,[3] in which I described numerous cases of claimed heavenly messages which I found credible, including those of Divine Innocence, because they all tended to a similar content, essentially that contemporary society was neglecting its Creator and needed to be reconciled to him if it wanted to find a solution to its spiritual, moral and even political problems. I came to understand that Patricia's experience and the associated messages were so important that every effort was justified to make them known to a wider public.

Patricia Warburton Adamson was born in Bristol on 4th March 1940, the youngest of six children of a family of shopkeepers and business people who belonged to the Salvation Army. Her father joined the RAF during the war, and the family home was bombed, causing the children to be evacuated to different families. Towards the end of the war the family was reunited and went to live in Blackpool, where Patricia began school. She was sent as a young child to Salvation Army services, and later attended Methodist, Baptist and Anglican churches. Prejudice against Catholics was very much part of her background. She attended a Protestant Sunday school, heard the Bible stories and learnt the hymns. It was while singing the hymn *'There is a green hill far away'* that Patricia as a child saw a vision of Jesus crucified. She remembers feeling deep sorrow for Jesus on the Cross.

---

3    Dudley Plunkett, *Heaven Wants to be Heard* (Leominster: Gracewing, 1997).

Once she saw a procession of first Holy Communion children at the local Catholic school, with the girls in white dresses, veils and gloves, and carrying white prayer books. She longed to be like them. Being warned that if she ever entered a Catholic church there would be dire consequences only made her more interested in seeing inside a Catholic church. One day she achieved this and remembers standing next to a large statue of the Sacred Heart wondering why the heart of Jesus was shown outside his body. She told no one that she had entered this forbidden territory.

When she was eighteen Patricia left England for Canada to join her eldest brother. She worked as an au pair for two years and then joined an insurance company and did general office work. Being artistic and dyslexic, she found this difficult and boring. Her real interest was art and she studied commercial illustration and moved to New York at the age of 21, first to work and later to study Art and Fashion Illustration.

While in New York she met Antonio de Menezes, a Catholic from Goa. Later she returned to England and worked as an advertising copywriter for a women's magazine. She met up with Antonio again. He had come to work in the BBC monitoring service based at Caversham Park, near Reading. Later, in 1975, he worked as head of the BBC Portuguese Section, their foreign language radio service based in London. Patricia and he were married at Our Lady of Victories Catholic Church in Kensington, London. The priest who married them asked Patricia if she would allow any children to be brought up in the Catholic Faith, and she agreed to this.

Her eldest son, Subash, was born in Reading and was baptised in the Catholic Church of English Martyrs in that town.

*Patricia.* I was not able to forget my promise to have the children brought up as Catholics, but I didn't know how Catholic children were instructed, so the priest put me in touch with a religious sister in the parish who explained baptism and some areas of the faith to me. I mentioned my desire to be baptised and this was taken to mean I wanted to be Catholic.

Patricia felt a growing desire to be baptised.

*Patricia.* I wasn't really thinking of becoming a Catholic, I just wanted to be baptised. I had not understood how uninformed I was about the Catholic Faith. I just believed in Jesus and wanted to be baptised and that was it! After this the Sister instructing me led me towards Confirmation and I was confirmed one year later but again I didn't fully understand the Catholic teaching. When I was asked what saint's name I had chosen for my Confirmation I just said simply, 'I don't know any saints.' So, Sister Julian, who was instructing me, said, 'Then take Our Lady's name, Mary.'

One day, Patricia was riding her bicycle to work through the countryside. As she was riding beside a field of ripe corn blowing in the wind she heard a loud and clear voice say: '*I am the Bread of Life*'. She knew that the voice was the voice of God and felt a great desire to find this Bread of Life and eat it, but she had no idea where it could be found.

*Patricia.* I gave up my office job and received a grant to study fashion design and jewellery design at Maidenhead College of Art. I obtained the Southern Regional Diploma with distinction, the Dorothy Perkins Scholarship and the Licentiateship of Society of Designer Craftsmen in 1970. I was offered a place at the Royal College of Art but my second child, a boy, was on the way and I felt I should be home with the children. I found it hard to refuse this opportunity but decided to work freelance making jewellery and selling it in London galleries, in Vogue and other magazines. During the seventies I was designing and writing for craft magazines and teaching jewellery and making other crafts. I later taught the foundation year students at Epsom College of Art, Surrey and I also wrote a book for Hamlyn, Crafts from the Countryside. By this time, we had moved to Surbiton, Surrey, as my husband was working in London for the BBC, and my third child, a girl, was born.

Patricia received further instruction in the faith from the nun who was helping the priest at St Raphael's Church in Kingston-upon-Thames. She still had a very unclear understanding of Catholic teaching.

*Patricia.* I thought Holy Communion, the Blessed Sacrament and the Eucharist were three different things. When told that I should spend some time before the tabernacle, I thought this very odd, as a tabernacle for a Protestant referred to a building or a tabernacle choir. Why one should spend time outside a building just looking at it made no sense, so I took the children to Mass on Sundays and simply copied what everyone else was doing. In order to get through the Mass, which I didn't understand and found boring, I would read Catholic Truth Society books from the church bookstall about the lives of the saints.

# Chapter Two

---oxxo---

# How the Mystical
# Experience Began

Patricia was in the habit of keeping a diary. She found that her journaling was taking on a new shape with unexpected insights that appeared in dialogue form as she worked out what at first she thought were her own thoughts, but later found to be a teaching that was being given. Eventually she became aware of a voice that she knew to be that of Jesus.

*Patricia.* I only heard his voice to begin with. I thought it a magnificent voice, with authority but kindness. I wasn't frightened. I didn't know Our Lord as I know him now, but I believed in him. I was always open to Jesus, but I was so ignorant.

Did you see him then?

*Patricia.* No, not immediately. I was hearing his voice
and also seeing various scenes as if I was part
of them. Contemplative prayer became an
intimate conversation with Our Lord, very
animated and real; I was taught about things
that I wouldn't have been able to think of and
I began to ask questions. Our Lord couldn't
give me everything all at once. He would
give me visual examples of the catechism, as
a teaching. Later I not only heard his voice
but saw images and visions that formed a
sequence of teachings of the faith and urged
me to take a new direction in my life.

I was beginning to pray a lot more than
I had before. I still didn't understand the
Catholic faith, which was why Our Lord gave
me visual aids to enlighten my understanding.
I saw a river of life flowing from the side of
Christ. It appeared as a real river that one
could hear and see. It made all things new
wherever it flowed. I wanted to refresh myself
in it and drink this pure life-giving water.
It was amazingly vivid. The messages began
at first once or twice a week, and then they
became daily. Some have said that I got these
ideas from the Bible, but I didn't read the
Bible which I only knew from mindlessly
copying out texts at school as punishment for
misbehaviour, so I actually disliked the Bible.

In 1984, after I had been receiving the inspiration for some time, I met Fr O'Hanlon, a curate in a neighbouring parish. I hadn't shared my experiences with anyone until that point. When I told him I was receiving this inspiration he refused to believe me. Our Lord asked me to give some of the messages to him. He said, 'If you do I'll throw them away', and he did, but Our Lord said to still give them to him. After a while Fr O'Hanlon spoke to another priest who said he shouldn't throw the messages away and that he thought there was something important in them.

Fr O'Hanlon invited me to a Rosary group. I hadn't prayed the Rosary before, and I was very suspicious of the people who were kneeling and chanting repetitive prayers. I was so nervous I didn't even listen to the words of the Rosary. I believed in just praying to Jesus, and I thought this might be displeasing to him. At the time, I had no devotion to the Mother of God and I knew nothing about the saints. The first saint I learnt about was St Anthony, who I was told found things that one had lost. I discovered he certainly did find mislaid items. He was the only saint I prayed to! Later I learnt not to just read about the lives of the saints who lived in the past but also to pray to them and ask for their intercession.

There came a time when Fr O'Hanlon said he believed I was receiving a special grace.

This was a great relief for me but it caused him difficulties with his parish priest who was sceptical. Father began reading the messages and taking notice of their content. Some of the people in the prayer group I attended became the nucleus of the Community of Divine Innocence.

Fr O'Hanlon suggested to Patricia that she make a consecration of her life to Our Lady; he told her that Our Lady would take care of her. Soon after this, Heaven intervened, and Our Lady and Our Lord began to give the messages of Divine Innocence and to teach her the Faith in a much more rigorous way.

*Patricia.* One day Our Lady appeared to me in my house. I was making clothes for my children. She said, 'Just as you are making clothes for your children, I want to give you a new robe of innocence.' At that time, I did not know that this new robe of innocence was via the Sacraments and the teachings of the Church. The new robe of innocence was Christ's Divine Innocence living and triumphant in me. Our Lady said, 'You are like an orphan, I know you but you do not know me, and there are millions like you.' At the time, I knew she was Mary, Jesus' mother. I just called her Mary. I noticed that Fr O'Hanlon used more respectful names, such as Our Blessed Lady or Mother of God. I remember once in Medjugorje, when I was dressed for the heat, a priest said Our Lady would not appear to someone dressed like that! Our Lady was so kindly and would just look at what I was wearing, and I would know I should wear something more modest.

You seem to have some infused knowledge and understanding of what you are seeing?

*Patricia.* Many things are being shown at once. For example, a vision might be shown, with infused knowledge to accompany it. I could ask questions and explanations were given. I was conscious of my own shortcomings, but Our Lord and Our Lady were gentle and loving. Sometimes there would be a reprimand.

Why do you think that Our Lord chose you to give these messages?

*Patricia.* Once Our Lord said it was not because of merit but because of need and there were many other souls who needed this grace. At another time, I was shown a girl sitting by the side of the road who was dressed in poor ragged clothes. This was the state of my spiritual life because I did not know the full Catholic truths, and also because of the way I had been treated in life. It was made

known to me what Our Lord was thinking as
he looked at this girl:

*Jesus.*   If I can restore this wretched soul, and the
suffering she has been through and the
way she has been treated, everyone will be
encouraged.

*Patricia.* He needed someone who was not Catholic,
who had a background of animosity towards
Catholics, who was ignorant of the Faith,
someone who had gone out into the world
at sixteen and led a wild artistic life, but also
a kind of innocence that had been crucified.

So, you are coming to know Jesus and Mary as persons.
How did your relationship to them alter?

*Patricia.* With Our Lord, it became a love-relationship
in the soul, knowing him in a more personal
way. One can still receive a reprimand from
Our Lord. At times, I was being too forward,
with not enough spiritual finesse. He would
say come to his heart through Our Lady's
heart, because she can help the soul to be
more delicate in the way it draws close to
Our Lord. At the same time, there is no
restriction upon the soul; you can fly to him
when you need to. He is so good to us and
wants us to have an intimate, happy and
relaxed relationship with him.

And did the kind of messages you were receiving change?

*Patricia.* The messages began to take the form of instructional visions and interior locutions. Many of the visions were a vivid, visual catechism. Some of the messages are of a universal character for the Catholic Church; others are more personal. They are an amazing instruction for my spiritual formation or for my particular situation, for example in the family where there are special challenges. Our Lord said that what he gave to me he gave to everyone and the Way of Christ's Divine Innocence and the Novitiate of the Holy Family would help all people.

One day, while attending Mass, Patricia had a life-changing experience. It seemed to her that she was holding the divine infant Jesus in her arms and he was speaking to her about the ceremony taking place. While the Scripture passages were being read he said to her, '*I am this Word*'. Then, he pointed to the tabernacle and said, '*I AM the Word made flesh*'. When the time for the consecration approached, he said '*I must go now to be born upon the altar*'. This led Patricia to understand, as she had not until that moment known, that it was the incarnate Jesus who comes in word and flesh in the Mass, and that he was truly present in the Blessed Sacrament reserved in the tabernacle. She experienced a supernatural faith and was able to accept that she was becoming a divine instrument in Heaven's work of restoring faith and goodness in a very nearly godless society.

*Patricia.* The visions happened in many different places. For about two years, no one knew about these experiences as I felt they were personal. At first, I did not tell people or my family what was happening but little by little things came out into the open. Our Lady showed me that this gift was for everyone and for the whole Church.

Were the messages given by dictation or did you recall them afterwards?

*Patricia.* Mostly by dictation and visions. Later Our Lady began to appear at some of the prayer group meetings and we would say a prayer of welcome and then I began to write down Our Lady's or Our Lord's teaching. Some of the early messages are undated or still in the handwritten form. The aim is to compile all the messages. It is difficult because they are words, scenes, and instruction which are awkward to record. I used to say, 'I am being shown...'. We were not experts in collating all this interaction that was in conversational style. The messages are now being gathered together according to themes.

Patricia was receiving the messages, but others were caught up in the events and began to promote them.

*Patricia.* We asked the Archbishop for permission to form a Private Pious Association but we received a letter from him saying we did not need permission. Some group members formed a charitable trust and edited the messages for a simple newsletter. Our Lord asked that the first Church of Triumphant and Crucified Innocence should be built in England and asked us to acquire the land on which Manor House Convent and School had stood. Our Lord showed that if every Catholic in this country were to give only one pound the land could have been acquired. However not enough funds could be raised to acquire the land and permission was given to the developers to build houses and flats. Our Lord said to acquire two of the houses, and this has been achieved with the help of divine providence and generous benefactors. Hundreds of people came for the Community's prayer days and processions, but the local churches discouraged them. Fr O'Hanlon was moved to another parish and things got more difficult.

There were other priests and theologians who were kind and helpful at different times, and Patricia maintains contact with priests who give her advice.

# Chapter Three

---❦---

# The Impact of the Revelations on Patricia's Life

At one point the fact that Patricia was a person receiving private revelations was disclosed, perhaps by a member of the prayer group, and this led to publicity in the media. Antonio only learnt about the visions his wife was having through a news report at the BBC where he was working. People were stopping the children at school to ask them about their mother. Reporters called at the house and questioned Subash, her eldest son, a 14-year-old at the time, but only looking for a sensational angle.

*Patricia.* It was miserable, but the messages were pushing me into the open, and this was uncomfortable for me and for others; if you read the messages you can see that I could not have invented them.

Later, did people become interested, respectful?

*Patricia.* Those with open minds were interested and respected the grace but, on another level, things went on getting worse. Among family and friends, it is often embarrassing and awkward to talk about the faith and the private revelation. God leaves the will free and one must respect that. Anyone with good sense does not seek these experiences but what you believe to be the truth you must accept. You have to juggle this experience with everyday life; often it's not very easy and also you are dealing with people who think you are crazy or who don't understand, so you must keep your feet on the ground and just get on with the work at hand.

The teachings in the inspiration that Our Lord was revealing are beautiful, and that kept me going. But there were also visions that were quite horrific, where you were being taught what crucified innocence really is. In all the areas of one's life Our Lord proceeded to help all who responded to grow in the faith and learn how to walk in the Way of his Divine Innocence. Little by little, the crucified innocence in people's lives is healed, and they grow in innocence according to the Gospel and the teachings of the Catholic Church.

Were you still working at this time?

*Patricia.* I worked at home freelance, and also once or
twice a month for the Goldsmith Company,
teaching training instructors jewellery and
other crafts. My jewellery was becoming
more spiritual. I wanted to explore Catholic
religious themes and symbolism in my work
and this I did working in a combination of
gold, silver, ceramic, coral, fabric and various
other materials. I was interested in the fact
that all these materials were gifts from God
and one should give him glory in one's work.

As Patricia's knowledge of the faith deepened so did her
understanding of the theological and doctrinal content
of the messages. The Lord followed a specific teaching
programme, and grace gave her a hunger for the Bread of
Life. She was drawn to the Sacraments of Confession and
Holy Communion, to the Mass and Catholic devotions.
Later, the Lord asked her to begin saying the Rosary and
the Divine Office, and to study the *Catechism of the Catholic
Church*. Eventually she studied theology in a formal way,
and with others in the Community she obtained a BA
Divinity degree and continued with an MA in Pastoral and
Educational Studies.

*Patricia.* A very important part of the Divine
Innocence Community life is the ongoing
study of the faith. Our Lord encouraged us
all to learn a little more about the faith each

day. Commenting on a popular saying he remarked, '*Ignorance is not bliss, it is ignorance and leads to heresy and error.*'

## The Effect on her Spiritual and Prayer Life

When asked what effect experiencing these divine revelations had on her spiritual and prayer life, Patricia gave a considered reply.

*Patricia.* My prayer life before this inspiration began was just my prayer to God and at times I wasn't sure if there was anyone listening. I remember asking God if he really existed could he reveal himself to me because I couldn't find him. I realised later that I had done what Our Lord had said in the Scriptures: 'Ask and you will receive.' God did reveal himself ever more deeply. I was shown the practical and spiritual benefits of an ordered prayer life and how one was strengthened through prayer with others. This was through the Mass, the Rosary and the Divine Office. My prayer life became less self-centred and because of that I benefited from the prayer of the Church and other Catholics and they in turn benefited from my prayers. I understood better the beauty and safety of a community of believers that is the Catholic Church.

Through saying the Divine Office – the

prayer of the Church – I lost my dislike of the Scriptures. I was shown the power and beauty of the Mass and was taught that it is the self-same Sacrifice as Calvary made present in our time, and how in the Mass all things are made new in Christ. When we bring our joys to the Mass our joy is made perfect in Christ. Our difficulties and sorrows and problems are eased because all sin and death has been destroyed by Christ on the Cross. The effectiveness of my prayer greatly expanded. The Mass is like an eternal new morning full of power and divine love.

I was taught about appropriation in my prayer and life. Appropriation means making something your own to help others and yourself. For example, I was shown I could appropriate Our Lord's infinite merits for the conversion of someone, or Our Lady's love of her divine Son so we can love him as she loves him. I began to appropriate the virtues of the members of the Holy Family for my family and all families. I became more confident in this new and infinitely expanded way of praying for the spiritual and temporal needs of myself and others.

Another fruit of this inspiration was the importance Our Lord placed on Confession. He encouraged frequent Confession and arranged that a priest who understood my situation was available for Confession. I was able to forgive others the sins they had committed against me and not to place myself above Our Lord who had forgiven me. Through this purification, weaknesses and sins were addressed. When Our Lord revealed the state of my soul, and the seriousness of my sins and my ignorance of the Catholic Faith, I was horrified and longed to change.

# Chapter Four

—◦◦◦—

# The Community of Divine Innocence

The Community of Divine Innocence was formed around Patricia at a time when the teaching was still at an early stage.

*Patricia.* Sometimes we misunderstood what was wanted. When Our Lord said he wanted an Order founded we thought he meant one of the traditional religious orders in the Church, such as the Jesuits or Benedictines. At that point, we hadn't grown enough in our understanding of the divine Order founded in the Holy Family and in the Church at the dawn of Christianity. We were directed to the original design of the Holy Family, which is Christ-centred, with the nurturing role of

Our Lady in all women and the protecting role of St Joseph in all men including priests, with all seeking to be Christ-like.

The Community was formed by those who put the messages into practice, in particular those who made the commitment to the Holy Family. In these people there was a growing awareness they were truly in the Holy Family; and this united them in an understanding that they were part of a worldwide community – the Family of Divine Innocence.

Jesus did not clarify every point of his teaching all at once. We were given time to nurture the Way of Divine Innocence in ourselves and others. Gradually, we came to understand Our Lord's intentions regarding the practical organisation of the work as we ourselves developed in the spirituality. We realised that what was needed was our 'yes' to Our Lord founding his original divine Order in each one of us. This meant that we needed to be open to allowing Christ's Divine Innocence to be triumphant in the female and motherly roles of all women and the male and fatherly roles of all men, including priests. This is better understood from within the Holy Family itself, where special graces are available to those who make a commitment to belong to it.

When Patricia was asked how the inspiration had affected her as a person who was being asked to take on a leadership role for which her life had not prepared her, she countered that when she was referred to as the foundress, she would say, 'No. *I'm not the foundress, Our Lady is.*'

*Patricia.* I didn't envisage being in charge of anything or founding a community. One day, when I was making the Stations of the Cross in St Raphael's Church, Kingston-upon-Thames, I heard Our Lord say, 'Found the Order of Divine Innocence.' I was so surprised that I looked behind me thinking that Our Lord must have meant someone else but there was no one there. I had little confidence that founding anything was possible.

Certain messages about respecting the motherhood of Patricia, particularly while acting for Our Lady as her daughter, could be applied equally to all women. Although, in the legal document establishing the trust of the Family of Divine Innocence, Patricia is referred to as the Mother-Foundress, she has accepted that her role essentially is as Mother of the Community.

For the present Patricia is envisaged as having the responsibility for clarifying the meaning of the messages, but in the future there must be a dual role of a mother and a father, to be elected; and decisions will be made by both together in a complementarity of roles. Whatever their state in life or their vocation, all in the community are called to a religious way of life because it is in the Holy Family that the Christian religious life was first lived. All Christian states of life are present in that foundational

Christian family. Each year, on the Feast of the Holy Family, they make or renew a formal Commitment to strive to be fitting members of the foundational Catholic Christian family in their separate or complementary male and female roles, according to their particular vocation as laity, religious or priests.

Two things were emphasised at this point: the commitment to the Community's prayers and devotions, centred on the Holy Family, and bringing to the Church authorities the request for the claiming of the victims of abortion as martyrs.

*Patricia.* We proceeded to try to carry out what we thought Our Lord wanted. With Fr O'Hanlon and other members, we made efforts to gain permission to found a community. We went to Rome to ask for guidance and advice from various Congregations and Pontifical Councils, including for the Family, the Laity, the Clergy and the Causes of Saints, for the martyr recognition of the aborted children. Fr O'Hanlon asked permission to head the community but was refused. Slowly a community was formed through reading, spreading the messages, prayers and devotions and the first prayer groups were very important in this. We moved forward in this way, sharing the inspiration with others in England and in other countries. We had inquiries from people, first Ireland, then from Belgium, France,

Australia, New Zealand, and the US, and later from Germany, Poland, India, Mexico and Africa. Each time a few people wanted to know more about the inspiration.

There was a growing response to Our Lord's request to make walks of reparation on the Feast of the Archangels (29th September) and the Holy Innocents (28th December), with the intention that all crucified innocence would be triumphant in Christ's Divine Innocence, and to remember the millions of children killed by abortion. A number of priests became interested in the messages and assisted us where they were able. They encouraged and supported us through their pastoral help and advice.

In the Catholic Church, there is a vital emphasis on the role of the priest, who stands in persona Christi, but there is little teaching on the important role of St Joseph within this priestly ministry. Priests will be more effective in their ministry if they understand their own part in the St Joseph role and the roles of Our Lady and St Joseph in the laity. We all need to begin where Christ himself began. Thirty years of Our Lord's life were spent in the Holy Family for a special reason. His mission is family-based. Our Lord invited his Apostles to come and see where he lived. The invitation is as new now as it was then. We can all learn to serve the very same novitiate that Our Lady and St Joseph served in Nazareth made universal in the Catholic Church.

Despite the enthusiasm for devotion to the Holy Family of many faithful in the wider community of the Church, there was also considerable resistance.

*Patricia.* We were attacked on various levels; one example was when Our Lord gave a message saying, '*I AM the Splendid Morning Star arising in a new age of Divine Innocence.*' (29/1/87) This was at the time of the New Age movement and we were accused of being new age, which is ridiculous because this inspiration concerns the original divine Order of the Holy Family and the Catholic Church. It includes a training programme to help us regain our lost innocence, not lose innocence to the degree that much of the New Age movement suffered. There are many wilted flower-power people who found that their new freedom from any sensible restraint in the areas of sex, distorted family arrangement and drugs did not bring happiness or peace.

Some people did not want to begin a training programme of deepening the knowledge of their Faith and having their devotion founded in solid Catholic doctrine. This would then sometimes turn to criticism or even mockery. One person said you could

not join the Community of Divine Innocence
unless you had a beard. I presume that was
not a requirement for the women! We were
accused of silly and serious things. None of
our accusers thought to check the facts.

Two significant developments occurred that gave a
shape and practical base to the Community. First was
the acquisition of the Foundation buildings, Nazareth
House, in Surbiton, where an office could be maintained
together with the daily prayer life of the Divine Office.
Later came the wonderful donation of Bethlehem Farm,
near Staplefield in Sussex, which became the location of
many Community devotions and activities, especially
those involving families.

*Patricia.* One concern was that we still had a large
debt on the Nazareth foundation houses.
I was troubled by the size of this debt. We
asked Our Lord to arrange to pay off the
house as a Christmas gift to Our Lady, and
just before Christmas a kind benefactor from
Ireland gave us the full amount, although
not knowing about the prayer. We have over
the years depended on a special member
of the Community, Kitty Fox, and her
childlike prayers. If she prays for something,
Our Lord seems unable to refuse her. She
is usually exact in her request to the pound
for important needs. She has complete
confidence that if we really need something,

spiritual or temporal, the members of the Holy Family will take care of everything. We have all seen miracles take place over the years.

We prayed for ten years for a Bethlehem House, but we did not have in mind a Bethlehem Farm until a very kind donor gave a farm to the Divine Innocence Foundation. We have always relied on divine providence for our needs and when I said to Our Lord we are hopeless at making money to run the farm, he told us to make hay and plant a garden, and to get on with sharing this way of life.

In following the pattern of the Holy Family, it is in Nazareth that Christ was conceived, in Bethlehem that he was born, and in Nazareth that he grew in stature and wisdom. In a spiritual sense, the same pattern is followed in us. As we are all different, the life of Christ, conceived, born or growing in us is different for each person. Our mission areas are different but in every walk of life, Christ, through the Novitiate of the Holy Family, can be conceived, born, and pursue his mission, suffering or triumphant in all areas of society. This way of life allows Christ and the Holy Family to reclaim the wastelands in our lives and transform them into fertile gardens of innocence and holy living.

# PART TWO

*Spiritual Insights Of The Way Of Divine Innocence*

# The Essential Teaching about Divine Innocence

When asked how the teaching she has received from Jesus, Mary and St Joseph was to be imparted to others, Patricia replied:

*Patricia.* I always thought the steps taken by the Child Jesus would be the way for beginners to access this teaching, and then to continue to follow him throughout his life, as he told us in the Gospel. He was conceived and grew in Our Lady's womb. He developed and was nurtured by Our Lady through her natural and spiritual motherhood under the protection and guardianship of St Joseph.

We learn our true Catholic Christian roles within the Holy Family, which Our Lord called the motherhouse of the Catholic

> Church. Our Lady is a type of the Mother
> Church, and her role in and through the
> Catholic Church is to show us how Christ's
> life is conceived, developed, born and grows
> in us so that we can walk in the way of Christ's
> Divine Innocence. (10/4/2017)

It was not at all obvious at the beginning what the full extent and implications of the messages of Divine Innocence would be. Indeed, they are still unfolding. One could compare this to the Gospels, where Jesus reveals his teaching in a gradual way. For example, he speaks in a veiled manner of his Resurrection, but this is so little understood that the apostles are dumbfounded when it actually occurs, and yet as St Paul says: '*If Christ has not been raised then our preaching is useless, and your believing it is useless*' (1 Cor 15:14), meaning that the Resurrection was the necessary corollary of his teaching. In the same way, though Jesus intended us to understand the vital importance of the Holy Family as the Church in miniature, offering Christians a safe home in which they could reach salvation, this would only gradually become apparent to Patricia and her associates as they progressed in their understanding of the Lord's teaching about the ordered life of the Holy Family and the Way of Divine Innocence within the Catholic Church.

*Patricia.* Our Lord did not immediately fully develop
each aspect of his teaching. He began with
'crucified innocence' and would take us as far
as he could according to our comprehension

and cooperation. He introduced the teaching about 'Our Lady of the Hidden and Mystical wounds' and related this to the hidden wounds in ourselves, our families and lives, and showed us the process of healing that could be found in the Sacraments of the Church and her teaching and in making the commitment to membership of the Holy Family. The different areas of the inspiration were gradually developed, like subjects at school. (9/1/2017)

The principal task facing the present writer was to make a synthesis of the messages which would convey their essence without betraying their great variety and depth. So, the plan became to include what might be considered the key elements to which an interested reader would need to pay attention as a first step in their acquaintance with the Way of Divine Innocence. If readers find that these messages speak to their hearts by God's grace, they are invited to seek further insight through the Divine Innocence website[1] or its publications.

The essential teaching of the Way of Divine Innocence according to Patricia's inspiration and to which adherence is proposed can be summarised in the following five points, which are not new doctrines but new or enhanced insights into immutable Catholic faith.

Jesus is the personification of the Divine Innocence of the Blessed Trinity made visible

---

4    See the Community's website: www.divineinnocence.org

within the Holy Family of Nazareth. In the coming of Jesus, we are shown the divine Order of the Catholic Christian roles of men, women and priests in the natural family and all family situations, including the family of mankind, the family of the parish, the family of the work place, and the family of nations, all called to be one holy family and people of God. When we move away from this divine Order we suffer or cause sufferings to others. The divine Order was established to help us all – men, women and children, wounded through sin – to regain our lost innocence, so that Christ's Divine Innocence can be triumphant in our crucified innocence (see Chapter 5).

We are all called to learn, through a detailed living Novitiate, to participate as members of the Holy Family, nurturing and protecting the life of Christ in ourselves and our vocation in the world (see Chapter 6).

In the Novitiate we have been given a rule of life. Many of its elements will be familiar to Catholics, except that it is comprehensive in nature, specifying not only particular prayers in which aspects of the spirituality are encapsulated, but also a formal commitment to strive to be fitting members of the Holy Family itself and a concerted effort to live fully the liturgy and Sacraments of the Church (see Chapter 7).

All are urged to prayerful and ongoing study of the Faith, especially at what Our Lord calls the Eucharistic University, that is in the company of Jesus truly present in the Blessed Sacrament (see Chapter 8).

A further distinctive feature of the Community of Divine Innocence is the mission it has been given to make reparation for the sin of abortion, and indeed for all sins against Holy Innocence, and to work for a deeper theological understanding of the role of the victims of abortion as companion martyrs of the Holy Innocents of Bethlehem, killed by Herod. And, finally, the Community is charged to appeal to the ecclesiastical authorities of the Catholic Church to recognise the martyr status of these children (see Chapter 9).

# Chapter Five

---∞∞∞---

# The Order of Divine Innocence in the Holy Family

The Order of Divine Innocence, founded by Christ in the Holy Family and the Church, is a living reality that came into earthly existence from the moment of the Incarnation and offers a deeper illumination in our time, when the forces of evil are striving as never before to destroy our baptismal innocence. It is the original and perfect Christian Order in which all religious orders of human foundation are summarised and contained, the 'whole diamond' of which every other foundation is a single facet. When Jesus first mentioned the Order of his Divine Innocence, Patricia did not understand his intention:

*Patricia.* Little by little, Our Lord showed us that he
had founded a divine Order, first of all in the
Holy Family and then, as time went on, in

the Church. It wasn't therefore a matter of establishing a new Order but, by co-operating with grace, given in our time and assenting to the divine Order that Christ had already founded, and that needed to be founded in us, in our vocation and in all peoples and nations. In this way, we become one universal family and people of God within the Catholic Church. (June 2017)

## The Holy Family of Nazareth

The Community of Divine Innocence attaches great importance to devotion not just to Jesus but to Mary and St Joseph who, through the life of the Holy Family of Nazareth, inspire virtue in our own lives and throughout the Church. Devotion to the Holy Family or to its members is anchored in the tradition of the Catholic Church and has found expression in limitless forms, including the liturgy, prayers, pious practices and art work, so that it is mirrored in the lives of the Church's faithful members everywhere. Nevertheless, it can be claimed that the Way of Divine Innocence gives a new impetus, and even a new sense of how such devotion is to be conceived and of the fruits to be expected of it. The Way of Divine Innocence is incarnational. We can see that this is so by reflecting further on Patricia's messages in the light of Catholic scriptural tradition.

The family, created by God in our first parents and destroyed by their sin, is restored in the Holy Family by Jesus, the Son of God Incarnate, and by Mary his mother and Joseph her spouse. Jesus redeems mankind through his Cross and his Divine Innocence living and active in them. Just as the motherly role and authority of Our Lady was given to her by God the Father, so too was the fatherly authority and role of guardian and protector given to St Joseph. Both Mary and St Joseph are God's instruments to help families to live according to the original Order that he founded and intended in the Holy Family, the Church and the whole family of mankind.

Although all people are children of God and are invited to be members of the Holy Family, many remain only '*distant relatives*', according to a message of Jesus on the Feast of the Holy Family, 2010, unless they are baptised in Christ and become his brothers and sisters and the spiritual children of Mary and St Joseph. That they are meant to have this close family relationship was confirmed by Jesus on the cross when he said to his mother, referring to the beloved disciple, '*Behold your son.*' (John 19:26) Furthermore, in the Mass of the Feast, the opening and closing prayers ask that we may imitate the Holy Family, and Pope St John Paul II also wrote powerfully of this family as a model for Christian life:

> *Through God's mysterious design, it was in that family that the Son of God spent long years of a hidden life. It is therefore the prototype and example for all Christian families. It was unique in the world. Its life was passed in anonymity and silence in a little town in Palestine. It underwent trials of poverty, persecution and exile. It glorified*

> *God in an incomparably exalted and pure way.
> And it will not fail to help Christian families
> – indeed, all the families in the world – to
> be faithful to their day-to-day duties, to bear
> the cares and tribulations of life, to be open
> and generous to the needs of others, and to
> fulfil with joy the plan of God in their regard.
> (Familiaris Consortio, para. 86)*

The Pope goes on to point out the qualities to be found in St Joseph and the Virgin Mary that are relevant to the functioning of the ordinary human family, the *'domestic Church'* (para. 61):

> *St Joseph was 'a just man', a tireless worker,
> the upright guardian of those entrusted to
> his care. May he always guard, protect and
> enlighten families. May the Virgin Mary,
> who is the Mother of the Church, also be the
> Mother of 'the Church of the home'. Thanks
> to her motherly aid, may each Christian
> family really become a 'little Church' in
> which the mystery of the Church of Christ
> is mirrored and given new life. May she, the
> Handmaid of the Lord, be an example of
> humble and generous acceptance of the will
> of God. May she, the Sorrowful Mother at
> the foot of the Cross, comfort the sufferings
> and dry the tears of those in distress because
> of the difficulties of their families. (Familiaris
> Consortio, para. 86)*

Speaking of the '*school of Nazareth*' Pope Paul VI had gone even further with his teaching, affirming that we do not merely imitate, but actually learn the virtues of Christian life by participation in the Holy Family:

> *Nazareth is the school in which we begin to understand the life of Jesus. It is the school of the Gospel. Here we learn to observe, to listen, to meditate, and to penetrate the profound and mysterious meaning of that simple, humble, and lovely manifestation of the Son of God. And perhaps we learn almost imperceptibly to imitate Him. Here we learn the method by which we can come to understand Christ... It is here, in this school, that one comes to grasp how necessary it is to be spiritually disciplined, if one wishes to follow the teachings of the Gospel and to become a follower of Christ. Oh, how we would like to repeat, so close to Mary, our introduction to the genuine knowledge of the meaning of life, and to the higher wisdom of divine truth!*
> *(Homily,* at Nazareth, 5 January 1964*)*

The Way of Divine Innocence, whilst reflecting this papal teaching, brings a grace that helps to fulfil the practical implications that follow for Christians from being members of the Holy Family, not merely following it as a model.

*Jesus.* When will mankind see their blood relationship to Me and truly become My brothers, My sisters and My mother, protecting My Holy Childlike Innocence in themselves and in others, living out this gift I offer to all men and women to protect, and to father and mother Divine Innocence in the family, their place of work and in their environment? (13/4/1989)

As brothers of Jesus we stand to inherit his kingdom of eternal life. We are to live as faithful children of Mary and Joseph, obedient to them as Jesus was, and fulfilling the commandments given to us by the Father, living according to his will and seeking to be perfect as he is perfect.[5] Patricia records Jesus' teaching about his family, its relationship to the Blessed Trinity and the triumph of Divine Innocence:

*Jesus.* If you look closely at this family you will see that everything is here, the unity and peace of the Blessed Trinity, the Father's will carried out to perfection, all the gifts and fruits of the Holy Spirit Triumphant in Holy and Divine Innocence, the one priest, Prophet, Priest and King, the perfection of the role of women and the perfection of the role of men. A new heaven and a new earth. The song of divine love sung to perfection.[6] (11/1/94)

---

5    The 'Prayer on rising' of the Community of Divine Innocence expresses this intention:
     *I rise for the love of Jesus and kneel at the altar of Our Blessed Lady's knee under the protection of St Joseph and in the company of the Holy Child Jesus. I ask you dear Jesus, Holy Mother and St Joseph to dispose this day for God's glory and my spiritual growth. I ask you to train me in the Way of Divine Innocence, so I become more like the Holy Child each day.*
6    Family of Divine Innocence, *The Song of Love* (1994).

## Jesus, Manifestation of the Divine Innocence of the Holy Trinity

The Son of God incarnate joins to his human nature not just his Divine Innocence but the Divine Innocence of the Blessed Trinity. Jesus teaches the Apostles about his Father and the Father's will and promises the Holy Spirit. On the Cross Christ took upon himself the whole weight of evil, taking away '*the sins of the world*'. (John 1:29) Christ was crucified by the forces of evil for love of us so as to be triumphant over sin and death. He reaches out to those who are crucified victims of sin to draw them into his Resurrection and to help them regain their lost innocence by faithfully following the Commandments, the Gospel and the teachings of the Church. In the messages, Jesus and Mary explain how everywhere our innocence and that of others is crucified – through broken marriages, abortion, social injustice, poverty, violence and abuse, the sins and circumstances of history, and all that is opposed to God's divine Order.

A further cause of crucified innocence which the messages highlight is our ignorance of, or failure to carry out in their fulness, the motherly and fatherly roles which are part of God's plan for mankind. With the coming of Christ, these roles have not only been restored but elevated to a dignity and importance that is most clearly seen in the Holy Family. The crucifixion, or wounding, of our true roles as men and women is partly because of the way they have been distorted by society, but mainly because of the wounds we receive through our own sins and the sins of others. Divine grace, obtained by the intercession of the Holy Family, leading to a greater awareness of the complementary nature and dignity of the motherly and fatherly roles of women and men, married or single, will ensure an environment that protects innocence and prevents it being crucified.

Jesus refers to the way that his innocence is crucified by our sins:

*Jesus.*    As I came to mankind in Bethlehem in littleness and innocence, to a pagan world full of sin and shame, so I come to this pagan world again in this age, in My Innocence, to touch the hearts and lives of men. I come to offer them My Innocence, to give them the treasures of the Eucharistic Hearts. Still I am turned away. Yet I am willing to come to the stable of your poverty-stricken lives to help you to enjoy the riches of My Innocence. Clothe yourselves in innocence – a new robe of innocence. Live and move and have your being in the Truth. I am dying in My brothers and sisters all over the world. Have pity on My Crucified Innocence! Set Me free! Set Me free! (July 1989)

Our Lady explained further how the Divine Innocence of Jesus can be spread to, or replicated in all of us:

*Our Lady.*    It is God's desire that Divine Innocence is made manifest in all mankind. You would have no idea how this is possible but for the manifestation of Jesus into this world. He has told you to follow him. He is your example,

but not only your example, he wants to live in
you in his Divine Innocence. (7/6/2013)

And in a heartfelt message, the Blessed Mother acclaims
the virtue of innocence:

*Our Lady.*     Innocence is more powerful in its
gentleness than the might of a thousand
armies with every weapon at their disposal.
Innocence, purity and holiness will win
the victory, by their very presence, without
violence of any sort. When the evil is so
malicious that it is determined to destroy,
then innocence will offer its very life as a
willing victim of Love for the glory of God
and for souls. (14/12/1986)

## Our Lady, Mother of the Hidden and Mystical Wounds

While referring frequently in the messages to his
*'Eucharistic Heart'*, Jesus also associates the heart of
his mother with the Eucharist through her hidden and
mystical wounds, as her thanksgiving, offering and
sacrifice.

*Jesus.*     Never will I forget those helpless hours on
the cross! And then deep within my Heart
I conceived the Age of Divine Innocence.
There, nailed to the Cross in agony for love of

you, was born a time where helplessness would be gathered into My Eucharistic Heart and become a force so powerful that evil and sin would be powerless against it.... The golden key that spoils all [Satan's] wicked plans. That golden key is the Mother of the Hidden and Mystical Wounds; through these Wounds and her Eucharistic Heart she has succeeded in unlocking the doors of My heart to you, My little apostles of the age of Holy Innocence. She alone crushes his head and releases the treasures of the united Eucharistic Hearts of Jesus and Mary. (1/3/1989)

*Patricia.* Our Blessed Lady has the deepest motherly concern for each one of us and for all her children wounded by the sins of history, circumstances and our own personal sin. Just as she suffered deep, hidden wounds, she knows of our hidden sufferings and has come to draw us to Christ to be healed by the Word of God and the Sacraments. Through her hidden and mystical suffering, Our Lady has obtained from God the Father this special grace for the Church and the whole human race. Our Lord and Our Lady wish to reach out to the most helpless victims of sin and teach them to make their suffering creative and redemptive in Jesus' passion, death and Resurrection. All women, married and single, have the motherly role of nurturing

the life of Christ in those with whom they
come in contact and who, like Our Lady,
often suffer a living crucifixion in their
wounded motherhood. (1/3/1989)

## St Joseph, Protector and Guardian of the Life of Christ on Earth

The frequently neglected role of St Joseph is brought into
great prominence in the messages of Divine Innocence.
The fatherly authority of St. Joseph, the foster father of
the divine child, is given to him by God the Father, from
whom all authority comes. The motherly authority of Our
Blessed Lady also comes from God the Father and that is
why Jesus was obedient to them, and why St Joseph has the
responsibility of being guardian and protector of the Holy
Family. Consequently, he is also the guardian and protector
of the Order of Divine Innocence, the extended Holy
Family containing all Christians. It is to him therefore that
we turn for his assistance in our spiritual and even material
needs, but even more it is to him that all men should turn
for guidance in their paternal roles and responsibilities.

*Our Lady.*     O my child, men and women have so
much to learn from the glorious Patriarch,
St Joseph! How privileged I felt to be under
his care and protection! When he understood
his sublime calling and the magnificence of
his role and the role of all men, married or
single, priest, laity or religious, his interior
joy was ecstatic. He gave his whole life in daily

toil and fidelity to fully realise his vocation as Guardian and Protector of the life of Jesus the Son of God. His role, and the role of all men, is to be Christ-like. To acquire a motherly heart which is sensitive to the needs of women, their security and protection, and their motherly grace. In this way the fatherly and motherly love of God came together in the person of St Joseph. (August 1994)

And Jesus underlines this special role of St Joseph in regard to men's behaviour and virtues:

*Jesus.* Men need to look at every area of their lives: their speech, their dress, their vocation, their attitude to each other, their attitude towards women and their relationship to God. Do they see Me and the Blessed Mother in all women and treat them as they would treat Me and the Blessed Mother? Do they see Me and St Joseph in other men? Do men strive to be Christ-like and to carry out the role of St Joseph in the world? Do they exercise the authority God the Father has entrusted to them, humbly and gently? (2/10/1997)

In her own life Patricia came to realise the importance of this teaching about the Holy Family.

*Patricia.* I learnt to trust in divine providence and God's care for me and all of us. I saw how much I needed Our Lady's motherly help and guidance in my own motherly and female role in my family and in the world, and how I could trust in the protection and guardianship of St Joseph.

## The Holy Family as Foundational Order

Jesus assured us that Mary is mother of all.

*Jesus.*    Even before I died I made provision for all mankind in my own home. 'Woman, behold your son... Behold your mother.' From that moment on, the whole of humanity, collectively and individually, had my mother as their own mother. (18/12/1996)

In an analogous way, St Joseph was given the mission of protecting and providing for Mary and Jesus in this world, but also, together with Jesus and Mary, of nurturing and protecting the life of Christ in each person made in God's image. The vehicle for this is in and through the Catholic Church, her Sacraments and teachings. This mission is Trinitarian. Through the Novitiate of the foundational Holy Family we are called to be Christ-like, to carry out the will of God the Father and to co-operate with the actions of the Holy Spirit, in order that our innocence can be restored in and through Christ's Divine Innocence.

\*\*\*

Many members of the Community of Divine Innocence recognise the spiritual power of the help they receive from responding to the invitation to participate in the living reality of the Holy Family, especially at a time when the family is under such attack.

- I believe the Way of Divine Innocence is a gift from heaven at a time when it is desperately needed. There is such chaos, disorder in family life, the correct roles of men and woman are distorted. Through the way of his Divine Innocence, Christ is restoring His original divine Order. (IS, England)
- My devotion and awareness of how close Our Lady and St Joseph are in helping and guiding me has grown. I see Our Lady and St Joseph as more than a wonderful example to be copied or as powerful saints, which they are, but I see them as being so real and active in my life because I believe in faith and feel that I am in their family. Personally, and in community work, I will start a practical task or project with a prayer to St Joseph or ask the guidance of the Holy Family. Although it seems to be a grace given it is also something that has to be cultivated, like the practice of the presence of God; it might be called the practice of the presence of the Holy Family. I would like to make my own the message which captures what I have truly experienced by living the Way of Divine Innocence, that the Holy Family is my 'real family home on earth and a living reality, a school for holiness, a refuge for believers and a help towards their salvation'. (SM, England)
- My eldest daughter had a baby out of wedlock and was

living with the father. She came home and participated in the First Friday Walk then went back to her boyfriend. Next day she rang me and said during the walk that she received the grace to 'come home'. She did, and for a year her boyfriend visited on weekends; she got involved in Divine Innocence; they eventually married in the Church and had 9 children. She became a member of Divine Innocence; later her husband was baptised into the Catholic Church and became a member as well. My youngest daughter's husband was in a bad way with drug addiction. I gave him the messages and prayers of Divine Innocence and told him to go to chapel and pray, which he did, and within 1 week he was completely free from drugs and still is for 9 years now. (BC, Australia)

- I have been enriched in all the messages have asked me to do; it is a growing sensitivity to Christ, a relationship with a context which is familial. I am under the care and providence of Our Lady and St Joseph; it is being Christ-like in a family. You have to foster the awareness, and all the messages help that awareness. Reading the messages and taking the Commitment enables us to come up close and understand Our Lord's family. (SM, England)

- I had resentment towards my father and was considering never talking to him again, but the mother of the Community, Patricia, often spoke about families and the way we can be a lifeline of grace to them, so I continued to visit him. Years later, before dying, he received the Sacraments of the Church. And the day of his death was August 17, the feast of the Mother of the Hidden Wounds. (MS, England)

# Chapter Six

The Novitiate of the Holy Family

The Holy Family offers a Novitiate through which all can *grow in stature and wisdom before God and men* (Luke 2:52), and participate in the childhood of Christ, in the very home where Jesus himself grew up. Again, this growth is not mere imitation, wonderful as that would be. It is something much more. There are messages referring to the way that believers can assimilate characteristics of the Holy Family. All Christians can find a new impulse towards holiness through this possibility of appropriating in prayer the Holy Family's qualities and virtues, especially their humility, obedience, love and courage. This leads us on to explore the universal nature of the Novitiate as Jesus revealed it.

*Jesus.*    My Innocent Childhood was safe in Nazareth. The perfect role of all men, women and priests came out of Nazareth. The Church came out of Nazareth and must return there if all the members are to live the perfection of my perfect design for the family, the family of mankind and the Church. Why do the priests not hear my invitation to come and see where I live? (John 1:39) The life of the Trinity in Nazareth is not dead; it is alive, active and vigorously universal! This grace is to transform individuals, families, the roles of men, women, children and priests; to renew the Church and the whole world. Go down to the Motherhouse of the Church and flow out as one Holy Family! The gifts and fruits of the Holy Spirit triumphant in you will renew the face of the earth! Oh, what a desert you live in, yet you could live in the New Garden of Eden! (11/12/1997)

In John's Gospel, Nathaniel asks, '*What good can come out of Nazareth?*' (John 1:46), but here Jesus has given a resounding reply. The word Motherhouse is significant. Religious orders usually have a Motherhouse. It is a foundational place, a centre and custodian of the original charism. The life of Nazareth is such a place, where the original Order for all communities, starting with the most fundamental, the family, was revealed. This life of Nazareth is now universal, and here an important new awareness is being given to the Church in this inspiration. But this truth is not only for the Church. Whatever the value of particular faiths as ways to God, Jesus is the universal redeemer and the Holy Family is the universal family.

Patricia posed an important question to Jesus: '*If it is through Christ and in the Holy Family that we can find our salvation, how exactly does this come about? What do we have to actually do? How can we live more perfectly the ordered life of the Holy Family?'* Jesus answered her in a detailed message which is quoted at length because of its special importance in revealing the value of the Novitiate for all Christian vocations:

*Jesus.* The first thing to remember is that the Blessed Mother and St Joseph were the first members of the Church and I Am the Head of the Church. All members of the Church are members of My Body. The Holy Family exists within the Church. The Apostolic mission of the Holy Family is that all humanity becomes one Holy Family and people of God, one flock under one Shepherd and one Lord, living one Faith within the Catholic Church. It is through a deeper understanding of the theology of the Holy Family, and serving the Novitiate of the Holy Family, that those outside the Church will see that the Holy Family, within the Catholic Church, is the divine Order I established at My first coming.

My act of redemption is not only for individuals but is family-based, the family of mankind. I established a divine Order in creation, in man and woman, in the family and in the Church. All belong to a family, but your true home on earth is the Holy Family, within the Catholic Church, and it will still be your home in heaven, the glorious Family of redeemed mankind triumphant in My Divine Innocence.

The role of motherhood has been redeemed. A Christian Catholic mother, like unto the Blessed Mother, must give birth to my life in all her actions, thoughts, words and intentions. She can only nurture my life in herself and in the world and in every vocation from within the safety of the Catholic Church I founded, not in any other foundation.

The fatherhood of man has been redeemed and, like unto St Joseph, Catholic Christian fatherhood is called to protect and guard my life in this world. All men, married, single and priest, must protect and guard my life in themselves, in others and in their particular vocation. They can only do this effectively if guided by the fullness of the Truth, in the Holy Family from within the Catholic Church. Everywhere you witness a divine Order of things. Do you think I would not reveal to you the divine Order of the family? Why did I spend so long living the divine Order of the Holy Family, the domestic Church now universal through the Catholic Church, if not to give you the example that you are all called to follow? (5/6/2009)

Living as members of the Holy Family means that we are not following a theoretical ideal but a living reality with which we can cooperate. So no longer do we live, but

Family camping holiday
Lancashire, circa 1949.
Patricia is dressed in the uniform of a Salvation
Army Sunbeam, third child from the right.

Patricia at Nazareth House
March 2018. Statue of the
Mother of the Hidden and
Mystical wounds in the
background.

Marriage of Patricia and Antonio at
Our Lady of Victories Catholic Church,
Kensington, London 1965.

Patricia, with the family of her eldest son, Subash, who has responded
with his wife Dymphna to the teaching within the messages by making
the Commitment to the Holy Family.

Fr.O'Hanlon explaining the spirituality of Divine Innocence to Pope John Paul II in 1987. His response was that this in an inspiration of the Marian year, and he gave his blessing on the aims. Patricia is just visible in the background with her daughter.

Early walk of Reparation outside
Our Lady Immaculate Church, Tolworth.

Nazareth House, 'This is the shrine of Nazareth Universal lived! It is the shrine of millions of aborted innocent children of all nations! It is the birthplace of the Eucharistic University and the gift of the understanding of the Novitiate of the Holy Family and the teaching of the Philosophy of Divine Love. From here special graces will flow out to the whole world.' (Words of Jesus, 21st June 2000).

Bethlehem Farm , a gathering on the 17th August for a procession, rosary and talk on the messages of Divine Innocence.

The statue of Our Lady being carried on the walk of Reparation. These walks are held each First Friday, and the Feasts of the Archangels and Holy Innocents.

People kneeling near the pine tree while a message is being given. Our Lady requested people to gather at 12 noon on week days and 9 p.m. on Saturday and Sunday to pray the Angelus, Credo, Magnificat and Rosary and also to give her their petitions.

Bethlehem Farm, 12 noon Rosary outside in the summer

Prudence the shire horse providing rides on 17th August, which is a
special family day at Bethlehem Farm to honour Our Lady, Mother of
the Hidden and Mystical Wounds.

Feast of the Holy Family 2007. Celebrating over ten years of the
Commitment to the Holy Family.

Patricia receiving her B.A. Divinity, after five years study at the
Maryvale Institute, Birmingham, from Archbishop Vincent Nichols.

Eucharistic
Medal worn
in honour of
Our Lord,
truly present
in the Blessed
Sacrament

Patricia's first drawing to
express the vision of Our
Lady, Mother of the Hidden
and Mystical Wounds.

The cross of our
crucified innocence

Statue made to show
Our Lady under this
new title.

Divine Innocence
triumphant in our
crucified innocence

Christ lives in us; we are called to be one Holy Family and people of God. The Way of Divine Innocence teaches that we are called to be trained and formed in love and obedience to the will of God the Father for our own eternal benefit and for that of the whole Church and all humanity. We bend our wills through self-discipline, and so bring our wounded or crucified innocence to the Holy Family to be restored through Christ's Divine Innocence and to be saved by his triumph on the Cross. [7] The Lord shares his Trinitarian love and glory with his creation, and with each soul that utters its 'fiat' (yes) with Mary.

Sharing the life of the Holy Family in prayer, and seeking their advice and help over every thought and action, we open ourselves to grace and to their wisdom and counsel. This is nothing less than the foundational spirituality of the Catholic Church. All vocations can be enhanced by this deeper understanding of divine Revelation, which cannot be at variance with any Catholic community or spirituality.

***

A Community member provided an ecstatic commendation of the Way of Divine Innocence.

- The difference the messages of Divine Innocence have made in my life is nothing short of exquisite.
  Beauty personified!

---

7   The daily 'Foundation prayer' of the community makes this request: '*Dear Lord, dear Blessed Mother, St Joseph, found the Order of Divine Innocence and the Novitiate of the Holy Family more and more perfectly in me every day in all the perfection of the original design of the First Christian Order.*'

An extraordinary awareness of my role as a man and father in society. The sublime role that St Joseph still carries out in the world, that of teaching men to strive to protect the life of Christ in themselves, in women and in their vocation. This is what Our Lord, St Joseph and Our Lady are inviting me to participate in.

I understand better that the role of women, be they married or single, is to learn to carry out Our Lady's role in the world, striving to nurture the life of Christ in themselves and in others. The roles of Our Lord, Our Lady and St. Joseph need to live and be active in us all.

I am aware that priests need to understand not only their role in the person of Christ but also the role of St. Joseph in their ministry with regards to the laity. They also need to protect the life of Christ in themselves and in the laity. They need Our Lady to teach them to have motherly hearts so they are sensitive to and able to co-operate with the role of women.

How Our Lord implores us to come before him in the tabernacle to enjoy an intimate relationship with him.

And the true meaning of what really is happening before us in the Holy Sacrifice of the Mass.

The beautiful teaching of the 'Song of Love', how we are being trained to accept our weaknesses. to understand humility and allow God to take me, my soul, on the journey to the high mountains of perfection.

At times you feel your heart could leap for joy out of its chest cavity!

Yes, everything is in this Novitiate. You don't need any other devotions except the Holy Family, the Order of all orders! (RB, Australia)

Others expressed similar ideas.

- We have experienced this amazing grace of the Way of Divine Innocence and the Novitiate of the Holy Family in action and personally I believe without a doubt that Divine Innocence will be triumphant in all the crucified innocence in the family, in the Church and in the world if we seriously make the commitment. It is a gift from heaven for these times. (JL, Australia)
- Everything I experienced, good or bad, was prepared by God and helped my spiritual growth. The deep teachings of the Truth given to Divine Innocence console, heal, encourage, so I am always looking forward to reading new messages. I thank God for the great mission and grace given to me within the Divine Innocence Family, and am so grateful I can live my spiritual life in love and peace, supported by the Holy Family so that I feel safe and happy within it. (SA, Japan)
- What has grown over the years while striving to live the Novitiate of the Holy Family is the realisation that it is a real training. It was in the messages and obvious, as a Novitiate is a time of training, but my initial focus and attraction was I wanted to be in the Holy Family in a more committed way. The training was in two ways. First by carrying out the obligations, like going to Mass and Confession more often, Eucharistic Adoration, regular study of Church teaching and the scriptures, all had a transforming effect; second through reading the messages and saying the prayers of Divine Innocence I have also noticed a growing spiritual sensitivity in a number of areas. (SM, England)

## The Novitiate Training

A programme of training has been set out in the messages for all those embarking on the Way of Divine Innocence. It is rooted in the sacramental and devotional life of the Church and is enriched by the spirituality of Divine Innocence as revealed in this grace. It is to be noted, however, that this is not a new doctrine, but essentially a working out of the fuller implications of the Papal teaching cited earlier. It has been described by Our Lord as *a greater light of the Holy Spirit on public revelation* (7/4/1997), whereby the life of the Holy Family of Nazareth is identified as the foundational pattern for every vocation that is in harmony with Catholic Christian teaching.

*Jesus.*    Pope Paul VI tells you that the home of Nazareth is a 'school'; in a school one is taught and one learns. In Nazareth Universal, you are taught to live in innocence through the Gospel, Sacred Scripture, and the teachings of the Church, with the help of the Sacraments. Such a training in holiness is a Novitiate for a religious way of life for all peoples. The Way of My Divine Innocence within the Holy Family and the Church is the Way of Perfection. (5/6/2009)

Patricia reviews how, for her personally, the Novitiate evolved gradually and in often surprising ways:

*Patricia.*  Our Lord has said that the Novitiate of the Holy Family is a lifelong process of growth in holiness. The members of the Holy Family are giving us a training that is rooted in the Sacraments and teaching of the Church. We were required to be diligent in the study of our faith. Our Lord (in my own case) began with a general Confession and then asked for a complete amendment of life in obedience to the Gospel and Church teaching.

I did not even know the Apostles' Creed at the beginning, and little or nothing about the Faith or Catholic practice and devotion. I was asked by a priest to begin to say the Rosary which he put on tape, and I learnt the Hail Marys and the Rosary format in that way first. I could see that others had a devotion to Our Blessed Lady, but I felt I did not know her and I mentioned this to the priest. He recommended that I make a consecration to Our Lady and she would do the rest; this I did, and Our Lady certainly stepped up my training. (July 2000)

While the primary value of the Novitiate is the salvation of an individual soul, it has the concomitant value of raising awareness of all the God-given blessings and benefits that constitute the Good News to be passed on to others for their greater knowledge and for their salvation.

*Patricia.* Our own awareness has been heightened, for example, regarding the importance of innocence, the need for Confession, the motherly and fatherly roles to be lived in all aspects of life, what Our Lord calls the Philosophy of Divine Love, and the wonder of our being able to appropriate the love of Jesus for his mother and for all mankind. We have to share with the Church all these things we hadn't heard of before. (31/7/2017)

# Chapter Seven

---

# The Rule of Life of the Community

With her evolving experience, Patricia was very much on the receiving end of the training. The Community followed in her footsteps. Guided by Our Lord, they used the Benedictine Rule as a guide, and this gave a shape to their community life. For example, the Rule shows how the role of a priest does not imply his authority in the Community. This follows the pattern of the Holy Family. Christ in his childhood was obedient to two lay people and grew to maturity in his family, protected by his parents. The dynamic is one of the priest (Jesus) learning from the laity (Mary and St Joseph) and the laity learning from Christ, the priest. It is not therefore lay-led as such but involves mutual respect and cooperation with each other's roles.

Jesus emphasised that the foundational rule of a community's life is love, be it in the family, or in any vocation in the world or in the religious life. This is why Our Lord has said that the grace of Divine Innocence will not be at variance with any charism or way of life, and that it can only enhance them.

*Jesus.*   You are told in the Holy Father's [Pope Paul VI] address how necessary it is to have a rule of life. I have given you the rule of love. Your God is Love, Divine Love, not the distorted presentation of a lesser love the world presents to poor souls starved of love. (5/6/2009)

## Confession, Holy Mass, and the Divine Office

The spirituality of the Way of Divine Innocence has many familiar Catholic features, including the Eucharist and the other Sacraments. Indeed, because the Holy Family is the Church in miniature, the Novitiate is at the service of the Sacraments of all.

*Our Lady.*   Live each day with the Word, the Scriptures, the Divine Office, the Mass and the Sacraments. (Feast of the Holy Family, 1990)

*Patricia.* We found frequent Confession a necessity because we are all weak and in need of the strength we receive from this beautiful Sacrament. Our Lord is always there, ready to help us. Early in the messages I went to Confession and I saw the blood of Our Lord wash over me and then spill onto the floor of the confessional and was shown that many did not appreciate that Our Lord poured out his Blood for all mankind on the Cross. One can see in the following that Our Lord mentioned this experience.

*Jesus.* See how, in Confession, My Blood washed over you and the excess ran even onto the floor. This excess is the excess of My Mercy that you are to take into the world in the form of forgiveness to those around you. Forgive, forgive, and continue to forgive, as I continue to forgive you. Why, men, do you continue to despise this great gift I have given you? Make full use of My Mercy in frequent Confession and Holy Mass. How else can I show you My Love and Mercy? Let Me embrace you in these gifts of Myself. (2/8/1985)

*Patricia.* After I had received absolution, Our Lord spoke of the proper disposition of the priest and people towards the Sacrament:

*Jesus.* The priest should consider people coming to Confession as those returning from the battlefield, some deeply wounded, some near to death, some with little hurts and others in psychological trauma. Children come to a good mother with their wounds and sinners come to their Mother the Church, which should not send them away but bend down and comfort them. Even when little ones come with small hurts and scratches, they need love and attention.

A good mother will tend little bruises and cuts with as much love as deeper wounds. She will correct gently where the children received wounds through their own fault and warn them of dangers. She will discern carefully where inexperience and wilfulness need to be checked. A good mother will draw the child to peace and reconciliation with the child's brothers, sisters and friends and set him on the right road again. The priest in Confession must be like this, showing to the penitents the Church's motherly love, care and instruction. This is what is meant by priests and all men praying for a motherly heart. This you can learn from the Blessed Mother. (8/4/2001)

The Eucharist, in the form of the sacred species, is the embodiment of Christ's Divine Innocence; the receiving of Holy Communion is the supreme moment when all can invite Divine Innocence to be triumphant in their crucified innocence.[8] This theme was expressed for Patricia in a particular vision she was granted:

*Patricia.* During Mass, at the words of the Consecration, I saw again a light, like the sun rising in the

---

8    The following prayer was given by Our Lord to be prayed often: '*O Divine Innocence, be triumphant in our crucified innocence.*'

early morning, as the Sacred Host was elevated. Then I saw a scene: a world in a perpetual state of a new morning. The light seemed to make the scene clearer as the words of the Consecration continued. I saw the light give life to the world and all Creation. I saw birds flying across the sky. In this scene I saw the Light of Christ giving life to the whole world. I had not really comprehended the words: 'I am the Light of the world', until today. I saw Christ giving light and life to the whole world through the priests and the Mass.

It is staggering to see the mystical power given to the priest. It is very difficult to put into words and perhaps I won't be able to explain, but the priest seemed to stand on a threshold between God and man. As priests offer the Holy Sacrifice of the Mass, they bring about an eternal new morning – forever new and life-giving. The priest has a special place between God and man. Once a priest, he has entry into this holy, mystical place. I can see, in a spiritual sense, a priest offering Mass. He is in a high place, to which his priesthood gives him the right to mount. (9/9/1988)

Another feature of Community life is praying the Divine Office:

*Patricia.* My own experience was that through the Divine Office, the prayer of the whole Church, the Scriptures flowed into me, teaching, reproving, guiding and strengthening me. The Divine Office seemed to express my joys and sorrows; it comforted me when I was sad or lonely; it calmed me when I felt angry or hurt and helped me to forgive and to seek reconciliation. God was speaking to me through his divine word and I was happy that I had persevered in learning the Divine Office. I was shown by the Holy Family that when this prayer of the Universal Church is said in the home it is like waves of a great sea flowing into the home and out again into the Universal Church, making them both one. (14/4/1994)

*Our Lady.*     By saying the Divine Office in the home you bring the whole Church into your home, and you take the family deep into the Universal Church. The Domestic Church becomes universal and the Universal Church becomes domestic in the intimate union of good Catholic families with the Universal Church. The family benefits from every Mass, every blessing, every prayer, every good work in the Universal Church. Every prayer, everything you do in the family, within the laws of God, helps to sanctify all the members of the Mother Church. (14/4/1994)

\*\*\*

Community members made the following comments on the Office:

- The messages of Divine Innocence brought order to my prayer life. They introduced me to the Divine Office, something which I probably would never have taken up if it wasn't asked for by Our Lord. I am still reciting my Office to this day; I would be lost without it. (AO'S, England)
- Although not really a practising Catholic, I was in the habit of praying morning and evening. It usually consisted of an Our Father, Hail Mary, and Glory be. However, I was going away to college and felt I needed something more. I observed that the Divine Office provided both structure but also variety, which appealed to me. I found it frustrating and annoying at times, worried I might be doing it wrong, but I did persevere and gradually it grew to be part of my routine. I believe that through saying the Divine Office I began to return to regular Sunday Mass and go to Confession again. (SM, England)

## The Community Prayers and Devotions

Jesus in the Eucharist is at the centre of the spirituality of the Community, and members are encouraged to attend Mass daily where possible. They are also asked to spend some time, again daily if possible, in Eucharistic adoration. A regular rhythm of prayer, undertaken in a spirit of adoration and reparation, is of vital importance. The Rosary and the Angelus are prayed daily. A Chaplet of Crucified Innocence is prayed to give special honour to Our Lord's Passion and death, the Hidden and Mystical Wounds of our Blessed Lady, and Christ's Divine Innocence. Other chaplets and prayers are intended to be prayed daily, and others in rotation.

Members of the Community were directed to wear a Eucharistic medal openly, in honour of Our Lord's real presence in the Blessed Sacrament, and to meditate on the picture on the medal and its meaning. Jesus also requested a double-sided cross to be made to provide a visible and easy-to-understand sign of his teaching concerning the triumph of Christ's Divine Innocence in our crucified innocence. On one side is a child crucified, wearing a crown of thorns, but no halo. This child is not Jesus but represents symbolically the crucifixion of our innocence and Christ crucified in us by our sins and the sins of others. The figure of the crucified child is also a striking image of the reality of the crucified innocence of children killed before birth.

*Jesus.*　The cross of the crucified innocence is you, gathered into My Innocence; your innocent sufferings gathered into My Innocent sufferings and united to Me in all your sufferings. (2/7/1985)

On the other side of the cross is a child with a halo, leaving the cross in triumph. This represents the risen innocence of Jesus triumphant in us, in our thoughts, words, actions, and intentions.

*Jesus.*   This image represents your pain, your loneliness, your wish that things had not turned out as they have, your desire for perfection, for peace, for love. Give Me your desires through this image, for a happy family life, for a tender and loving relationship, for peace and justice. Give Me your wounded bodies, your imprisoned hearts and minds. While imprisoned spiritually or physically, remember My Triumphant Innocence on the Cross, and I will remember your crucified innocence. (1/8/1985)

## Spiritual and Moral Guidance

All Christians are called to follow the Commandments and the teaching of the Church as exemplified in the life of the Holy Family for the triumph of Christ's Divine Innocence in themselves and in their lives.

*Jesus.*   It is My Will and command that you should regain your innocence through the teachings of the Church, follow the Gospel, live in Holy Innocence, and spread the spirit of Divine Innocence everywhere so that I may be triumphant in your crucified innocence.

*Our Lady.*   My children, when you enter the Holy Family by your Commitment, the Rules of the Holy Family apply to you. We lived by a holy discipline. No sin can exist within

this Family – no rebellious behaviour – no
disobedience to the Will of God and the
teachings of the One Holy Catholic Church
can come under my Motherly care. St Joseph
cannot be the guardian of sin, disobedience
or unholy behaviour. The Child Jesus is never
the companion of evil or sin. He is Innocence
Itself. He is sinless. He is Divine Innocence and
wishes to live in the company of His brothers
and sisters – those who strive daily to serve the
Novitiate of the Holy Family, by being docile
and obedient to the Commandments and
teachings of the Church and following Christ
in the Gospel. (Feast of the Holy Family, 1990)

Given the foundational status of the Order of Divine
Innocence, a question arises that was put to Patricia: has
this inspiration been offered previously to the Church, and
presumably not taken up, or if it has not been, why is it
being offered at this present time?

*Patricia.* Our Lord said it is the original Order for
humanity and the Church. It is in that
sense that it has been given earlier. There
are always areas where we do not take up or
put into practice the fullness of the Gospel
message, or we distort it through the effect
of other Christian denominations, religions
and philosophies that are not of the divine
Order founded by Christ. Concerning why
the inspiration is being offered now, Our

Lord said it was in preparation for his second coming. He wants to help prepare us so that he will find faith when he comes again.

## Eucharistic adoration

Eucharistic adoration draws attention to the beauty of the Blessed Sacrament, the body, blood, soul and divinity of Jesus in the host, white, pure, humble and entire, the presence of his love for all humanity.

*Patricia.* Very early in my conversion, a priest recommended that I spend time before the Blessed Sacrament and I was invited to an all night vigil. I remember saying to a priest, 'What do you do in the Church all that time?' I agreed to try it for ten minutes. The priest smiled and said 'Do not set limits on God. Come and see what happens.' I did, and to my amazement I stayed for the whole night and did not feel in the least bit tired and I enjoyed the silence and the times of prayer. I thought, this is easy, and had no idea that it was grace alone that had sustained me through the vigil. With confidence and pride, I went again the next month and fell asleep the moment I sat down. The grace had been removed to teach me humility, but little by little I began to look forward to the quiet contemplation and reading. I had discovered that one could have an intimate friendship and relationship with the Eucharistic Heart of Jesus in the Blessed Sacrament.

*Jesus.*    You can't imagine what joy you give Me by your presence. Do you know what it means to My Eucharistic Heart to have the company of the ones I love? When love is not satisfied, it pines for its love. You are My love – each soul on earth. You are here. You have come. What graces are being poured out on you! (11/7/1985)

*\*\*\**

Many Community members have found solace in Eucharistic adoration, as the following comment illustrates:

• To be baptised, then coming to know the spirituality of Divine Innocence, is such a grace. My life without knowing the existence of a true and living God changed into a life centred on the real presence of Our Lord in the Blessed Sacrament. (MT, Japan)

## Walks of Reparation

Reparation for our sins is a clear theme in the messages. It takes practical effect in the Lord's request for walks of reparation to be made by Community members, usually on a public route between two Catholic churches and barefoot where feasible. The messages deepen our understanding and appreciation of the value of loving reparation in union with Christ and lead us to more willingly accept the difficulties of life as a source of graces.

*Patricia.* We were shown that reparation in union with Christ is part of the Catholic Christian life. If all humanity is eventually to become one holy family and people of God, reparation is needed in sorrow for our own sins and the sins of the world, especially the sin of abortion where many thousands of innocent children are being killed every day. Public reparation is important, and we were requested to make walks of reparation, to express our sorrow for our own sins and for the sins of the world, on each first Friday of the month and on the feasts of the Archangels and the Holy Innocents.9

In 1988, Our Lord asked Kitty [a Community member] and me to make the first walk of reparation between two local churches, St Raphael's and Our Lady Immaculate, and there is a message that describes a heavenly procession that accompanied us on that walk. Little by little others followed, and the numbers of people coming on the walks of reparation grew, as did those reading the messages. At one point, St Raphael's was so full on a first Friday that the people were standing close

9 Every offence committed against justice and truth entails *the duty of reparation,* even if its author has been forgiven. When it is impossible publicly to make reparation for a wrong it must be made secretly (*Catechism of the Catholic Church*:2487).

behind those kneeling at the altar for Holy Communion.

Reparation is not confined to the special walks or chosen acts of penance. These are but a small part of our everyday lives. Rather it is the willing and loving acceptance of all our trials and sufferings, uniting them with the perfect reparation of Christ's Cross through the Holy Sacrifice of the Mass, that draws down grace on those in need. We should also offer all our joys and the good things that God gives us for the intentions of Our Lord's divine heart, through the Holy Mass wherever it is said throughout the world.

Our Lord and Our Lady have repeatedly asked for worldwide Masses of reparation, pardon and peace, in penance for our own sins and the sins of others, the sin of abortion and all sins against Holy Innocence. People may be troubled by serious sins other than those connected with abortion, for example, adultery, incest, homosexual acts, and alcoholism. By making these acts of reparation, victims can receive the grace to forgive and be reconciled with those who may be the cause of their injury. Perpetrators of serious sin can come to recognise the damage they have done to others and make atonement.

## The Commitment

It is thus a whole way of life that members of the Community of Divine Innocence decide upon, through a solemn annual Act of Commitment.

*Patricia.* The reason for the annual renewal is that we all slip back in various areas, or our circumstances change, and we need to take stock and consider how the Novitiate applies in new circumstances. We strive to make our lives Christ-centred and to spread the spirituality of the Novitiate. This is done by word and example. Jesus was the centre of the Holy Family in Nazareth. We consider Our Lady as our novice mistress and St Joseph our novice master and allow them to teach us to live daily the perfection of our motherly and fatherly roles, as seen in the lives of Our Lord, Our Lady, and St Joseph. On 6th March 2017, Our Lord said that '*The ordered life of the Holy Family is a teaching Order in itself.*' I felt this was very important.

Patricia added further details about the nature of the Commitment:

*Patricia.* A commitment is a free-will decision. We have seen that even children who wanted to take the Commitment and did so showed that it made a difference to their spiritual growth. Grace flows if the person is committed and not lazy about their Commitment. If they don't do their part and take the training seriously they simply stop growing in the understanding of the spiritual and practical life of the Holy Family. Then there is a danger of relating to the Holy Family only on a devotional level and at a distance, instead of allowing them to work in us and our lives. (6 /2/2017)

\*\*\*

Many members of the Community have found a new strength and consolation in the way they were able to change their lives through the Way of Divine Innocence and the Novitiate of the Holy Family:

- In 1991 a small group of 3 grandmothers – myself, 2 others and our very wounded teenage daughters – began to follow the Divine Innocence messages, and so began by doing the First Friday Mass and Walks of Reparation for the sins of abortion and all sins against Christ's Divine Innocence, learning the Community prayers, the Divine Office and the Rosary. Our girls had all attended Catholic Schools, and we had assumed that they were taught Catholicism, but when we started bible, scripture and catechism studies we soon realised how much the faith had been watered down and how little our daughters knew. But gradually over time these mothers received the grace to protect their children's faith and they all began to home-school their children, and so our prayer group grew into a prayer-playgroup with over 30 children. My daughter had 8 children. Another mother had 8 children and her husband became a Catholic and a member of Divine Innocence; a father of 6 came back to the faith; and a father of 3 received the Sacraments and became a member. (JL, Australia)

- In 2008 my wife left, and I was at my lowest. It was then that I looked up to the Lord for help. The advice from a family member of Divine Innocence to take the prayers and messages and sit in front of the Eucharistic Lord was providential, as within a week I was completely free of my drug addictions.... and to be honest I would not be in the Church but for the intercession of Our Lady of the Hidden and Mystical Wounds.... I believe this message of the Way of Divine Innocence is from God; it is so necessary for these times of broken homes and wounded children. (MC, Australia)

- When Divine Innocence came into my life I was married with two young children; my husband was not a committed Catholic and the changes after Vatican II caused some confusion, not that they came from Vatican II but from the conflicting interpretations put out. It was a time of unease and uncertainty, during which I clung to Our Lady. I did not study my faith or read Scripture except on occasion; this was before the *Catechism of the Catholic Church* was published. My faith was struggling. My marriage was a difficult one. Divine Innocence came like a dazzling light into the darkness, giving me strength and hope and guidance. The training in the Novitiate of the Holy Family helped me to see my correct role as wife and mother, and this made a difference in my relationship with my husband. Having a 'rule of life' with set prayers and study was a great source of security and strength for me. Through Our Lord's request to study our faith I did courses at the Maryvale Institute, something I did not think I was capable of. I found studying my faith before the Blessed Sacrament a great grace. (IS, England)

- The big change came in the desire to make the Commitment to the Holy Family. I realised it was a solemn thing. At first, I did not feel I was ready: 'Was I really committed?' 'Could I really put the obligations in place?' The Commitment to the Holy Family has brought order and structure to my spiritual life and this has helped me to order the practicalities of the day. When I order my day around the prayer and study of the Faith, the practicalities run more smoothly. (SM, England)

And from a Community member in Japan:

- I feel so confident and firm in my faith because I have been studying the Catechism and the Church teachings as a part of my commitment. For me the translation work of the Divine Innocence messages is like meditation and a healing process and the messages make me understand better God and myself. I am so happy that God gave me this work of living and spreading the messages of Divine Innocence, and I thank God for it. (MT, Japan)

## The Song of Love

The Lord gave a teaching called 'The Song of Love', a personal call to all to make the journey to the high mountains of perfection. The Song of Love is in the form of a prayerful dialogue between the soul and Jesus and Mary. All prayer, not only before the Blessed Sacrament but in the Divine Office, the liturgy and private devotions, unites believers with the Lord in a song of divine love. The entire essence of the messages is thus put into practice as a living spirituality.

This is illustrated by Patricia's conversations with Jesus, as presented in the Divine Innocence *Newsletters* and the book *The Song of Love*. It is made clear by these passages that it is not a question of our being spectators of somebody else's dialogue with the Lord; through *The Song of Love* we are to find encouragement to enter our own dialogue, and to learn directly from Jesus how he wants us to relate to him. *The Song of Love* gives a special insight into the Way of Divine Innocence. It is the soul's response in humility and silence to the training, the spiritual and moral guidance given in the messages, and to the grace and support obtained through the intercession of the Holy Family. Patricia herself found deep consolation in *The Song*.

*Patricia.* **The teaching of** *The Song of Love* **gave me a desire to make the spiritual journey to the high mountains of perfection. On this journey, there would be easy places to travel through, where one experienced the presence of Our Lord or Our Blessed Lady, but also difficult spiritual times when the soul was under attack from the forces of evil that would**

> suggest that there was no good in you and
> such a journey was hopeless, and you might
> as well give up and just enjoy life. I learnt that
> sin is not enjoyable, and the Way of Divine
> Innocence is true freedom in God's love, and
> a great adventure.

Fr Francis Frost [10], a theologian who worked closely with
the Community, characterised *The Song of Love* in the
following terms:

> *The dialogue form of The Song of Love awakens
> the reader to wanting to enter into this love-
> relationship too. Such was the technique of
> all the great teachers of the spiritual life: St
> Catherine of Siena, Thomas a Kempis, St
> Teresa of Avila, to name but a few. At the
> same time, it is the most ordinary of readers
> who is being given this invitation. Although
> the purifications spoken about reach to the
> depths of the soul, the language employed is
> very simple. It is also full of realism.*

*The Song of Love* is in the tradition of the biblical *Song of
Songs*, conveying God's love for the beloved, the soul.

*Jesus.*    Call other souls to enjoy My mercy. Love,
           mercy, peace, absolution and restored

---

10    An English Catholic priest who taught at the Faculty of Theology, at the
      Fédération Universitaire et Polytechnique de Lille and at the Catholic
      Seminary of Ars.

innocence flow like a mighty river from this side of mine. Tell poor souls wounded by so many sins to come and bathe in this river of divine love. Little soul, for you alone I would again bear all the pains of My passion and death were it necessary. Tell souls of the great love I have for each soul individually. (1/1/1991)

The themes of the dialogue often embrace moral and spiritual counsel, and are clearly Eucharistic, as on one occasion when Jesus said:

*Jesus.*  I am feeding you with myself to strengthen you. Do not be discouraged if those to whom I send you take a long time to respond. Do not give up if you do not see the light of hope come into their eyes. Be careful that so-called modesty and humility is not of the false kind and is really fear. False modesty is pride. Be careful that zeal is not really inordinate enthusiasm. Pride destroys true humility. Enthusiasm is like a firework, a spectacular display that soon falls dead to the ground.... Remember that it is fusion that gives lasting energy. Be fused and united to Me and then you cannot become spent of true zeal and strength, because you draw from living waters....

The *Song* is personal, and each soul will find they have their own special part; each individual arrangement and score is unique;

there is no other soul that can sing your part;
the symphony is not the same without you....
I wait with longing: will My love sing the song
I have composed for her?... The sound of her
soul's voice is on the breeze 'Thy will be done.
Thy will be done. My soul glorifies the Lord;
my spirit rejoices in God my Saviour – it is in
death that there is life' (death to self and death
to all that is not God). My love is coming. I
wait for her. I will clothe her in a new robe
of innocence and we will go to the high
mountains, singing in unison and in union
– together yet one – bathed in the sunlight of
My presence. (*The Song of Love*, March 1990)

There is also the theme of conversion of heart; the effect
of following *The Song of Love* is to bring the soul to
repentance and striving for perfection. Our Lord showed
Patricia in a vision the effects of the *Song* as they tried to
live and practice it.

*Patricia.* The effect the *Song* had on those who heard
it was strange: the *Song* which was filled
with compassion and mercy seemed to
affect those people who showed no mercy to
anyone; it seemed to have the power to melt
the hardest hearts and to turn bitterness
into joy; the song of humility and gentleness
turned proud souls to seek out the Master
Singer and beg him to teach them *The Song
of Love*; the song of joy and peace flowed over

souls who for years had lived in disunity and dissension and taught them to forgive and forget the wrongs of others. Only the *Song* mattered, and they for a time became lost in its beauty. *The Song of Love* seemed universal, yet personal, and made souls long for the high mountains of perfection. (22/11/1991)

When someone said they would like to rewrite the *Song of Love* to make it more understandable to children, Our Lord said, '*Don't change the Song; allow it to change you.*' (16/11/2016) Although it might seem that *The Song of Love* was to be understood as principally aimed at personal sanctification, it leads in fact to an opening to the world and its needs, both spiritual and material.

*Jesus.*  Now let me expand your Song of Silent Love to the utmost bounds of all the world!

*Patricia.* My Lord took me on a flight of love. When I thought of someone or some situation, he silenced my thoughts and instructed me to sweep the person or situation up in a silent wave of love, not my own frail love alone, but united to my Lord's divine Love pouring from the Eucharistic Heart of Jesus.

## The Philosophy of Divine Love

By his words, '*I am the way, the truth and the life*' (John 14:6), Jesus provides the surest foundation for philosophy, that is as the fruit of both faith, or Revelation, and reason. Scripture reveals that love is essential to our understanding of our existence and the existence of the world around us. The Way of Divine Innocence re-awakens us not only to the relationship of love between Creator and creature, as in *The Song of Love*, but also to the truth that Divine Love is the moving force of creation, the willing of being, and especially the willing of the human being made in God's image and likeness in mind, heart and soul.

*Patricia.* I was shown that the difference between the philosophy of Divine Love and other philosophies is that in other philosophies man tries to explain to man his being and existence and the reason for things. Man tries to penetrate these mysteries with his own intellect and reason and can only go so far. The grace of the philosophy of Divine Love has been given to show us that by reason and experience we can make the step of faith. Divine Love reaches down to man in Revelation, and out of God's love for mankind reveals himself and the extent of his love for his beloved children. Man is not alone in his enquiry into the divine mysteries. God is his helper, close at hand. (7/12/99)

Coming from an experience of God and leading to God, this philosophy is superior to all philosophies which come only from an experience of things and can therefore only lead us to things. This leaves the question of how God communicates such essential truths. For this, we must turn to Scripture, Church teaching and the person of Christ, '*in whom are hidden all the treasures of wisdom and knowledge*' (Col 2:3), and most particularly to our experience of his real presence in the Holy Eucharist, as the next chapter further explains.

# Chapter Eight

# The Eucharistic University and the Study of the Faith

Because of the neglect from which catechesis has suffered in the Church in the last fifty years, the messages of Divine Innocence give a needed reminder of the importance for Catholics of the study of their faith. Many Catholics are incapable of explaining or justifying their faith to unbelievers or even to other Christians. A remarkable feature of the rule of life followed by the Community of Divine Innocence is the 'Eucharistic University', or the practice of the prayerful study of the faith, including the scriptures and Church teaching, whilst praying in adoration before the Blessed Sacrament.

This has led to several Community members with little formal educational background excelling in academic study at degree as well as postgraduate levels. Like Mary in the Gospel, who chose the better part, they sit at the feet of Jesus to learn from him. (Luke 10:39)

*Patricia.* We were asked to study the faith and the Catechism and, for those who are able, theology and higher studies. We found this was much easier if we studied in the company of Our Lord's real presence in the Blessed Sacrament. Our Lord called this the 'Eucharistic University'. When we spend time with Christ in the Eucharist we should always begin with an examination of conscience and a prayer to the Holy Spirit for guidance.

We were shown that a new era of enlightenment can come about for those who submit their intelligence in humility to God, the source of all knowledge, and ask him to enlighten their minds and hearts through their systematic and diligent study of the faith before the Blessed Sacrament. If we study first for the glory of God and for the good of mankind and our neighbour, and not just to earn our living or through intellectual pride, God will bless our study and enlighten us in the most amazing way. (July 2000)

The light that shines forth from the Eucharist exposed on the altar is the Divine Love that illumines faith and imparts knowledge of both divine mysteries and the created universe. The Eucharistic University is the place where the Philosophy of Divine Love becomes clear.

*Jesus.* The Philosophy of Divine Love is the Alpha and Omega. It begins in God and ends in

God, has man for its subject, and creation to confirm it. The Rule of Necessity – your necessity is Divine Love! (30/12/99)

Study of this kind was specifically commanded by Jesus. On the first Friday of June 2017 speaking of the Eucharistic University Our Lord said:

*Jesus.* It is not just adoration, it is participation.

*Patricia.* It is more than adoration of Our Lord in the Blessed Sacrament. The Lord desires a relationship with the person seeking instruction in the Truth and enlightenment in their study of the faith, and also in their vocational subjects. Thus, they are able more effectively to help mankind, build up Christ's Church on earth and give glory to God.

Specifically, on study of the faith, Jesus said:

*Jesus.* The study of the faith is vital, and I expect the best results according to your intelligence and gifts. (13/5/1998)

*Patricia.* Our Lord showed that at university we are introduced to the faculty. Studying at the Eucharistic University means spending time with the Head of the Faculty, Our Lord himself, '...*in whom are hidden all the treasures of wisdom and knowledge*' (Col 2:3). He teaches us

> how to use our learning and talents according
> to the will of God, the laws of God, and the
> teaching of his Church. (5/5/1996)

The importance of the study of the faith is likewise strongly recommended by the Blessed Mother in several messages, for example:

*Our Lady.*    Defend your faith by studying it and knowing it well; it is lamentable that so many Catholics do not know their faith. So much time and effort are spent on useless pursuits, while you neglect your faith. Outward observance is not enough. You cannot live or defend your faith if you do not know it. How can you follow the gospel and the scriptures if you never pick up or study the scriptures? How can you know Jesus, if you do not look for him where he can be found – in the Word? (12/7/1994)

*Our Lady.*    Resolve today to begin or renew your study! Sloth is a deadly sin indeed when it comes to the knowledge of your faith. Take up the *Catechism of the Catholic Church*, the Scriptures, the Divine Office, the documents of the Church! (1/6/2001)

Patricia summarises the benefits of study at the Eucharistic University:

*Patricia:* When we spend time with Our Lord really present in the Blessed Sacrament and ask for enlightenment, we have available to us the knowledge of God. Who is the greatest healer of minds and bodies? Our Lord's miracles of healing and his power over sin and death are shown to us in the Gospels. Our Lord said that at the Eucharistic University he could teach any number of students, on any subject. Classes can be held locally and universally, as near as your local Catholic Church, and there are no fees to pay. The Spirit of Truth, the Holy Spirit, is available to help us in our studies. On the faculty of this University we have the help of all the saints in heaven. There was only one condition, and that was that those who were enlightened used the information for the glory of God, the good of mankind and the building up of the Church. (10/5/2017)

*Jesus.* The Novitiate of the Holy Family and the Philosophy of Divine Love studied at the Eucharistic University deepen the study of Catholic Christian doctrine and theology and is the way forward for the whole Church. (14/12/2004)

\*\*\*

Several Community members report how meaningful the study of the faith has become, and especially at the Eucharistic University:

- We know the importance of studying the Faith and often take our catechism and Bible and study before Our Lord's real presence in the Blessed Sacrament. We say the Rosary and we all go to Confession once a week where possible. (WS, England)
- I responded to Our Lord's and Our Lady's requests that we study in the Eucharistic University. When I started, I received permission to have a key to my parish church. The first course I did was the part-time three-year course at Maryvale on the Catechism of the Catholic Church, which I completed in the three years. I then went onto a BA in Applied Theology, part-time over six years, which included catechetical method and practice. I gained so much, which I am able to pass on in the catechesis in my parish, in RCIA, in the First Holy Communion and Reconciliation programme, and in Bible Study. (LG, England)
- I also met my future husband in Divine Innocence – we have now been married for 18 years, have five beautiful children (three of whom have special needs). My husband and I are staunchly pro-life and proud to be Catholic. Divine Innocence has shown us the importance of studying the Catholic Faith; the depth and beauty of it and the importance of teaching the faith to the children. Divine Innocence has inspired in me devotion to the Blessed Sacrament, including study before Our Lord's real presence (at the Eucharistic

University), and I was shown that both mother and child receive many graces if the mother, when pregnant, comes often before the Blessed Sacrament. (WS, England)

- The value of studying my Faith has been a major contribution in growing to love the Catholic Faith. I always had a hunger to know more about the Faith, but the encouragement of the messages of Divine Innocence has taken it to a higher level. First, the constant emphasis in the messages served to keep it at the forefront of my routine. Second, it was more than just spiritual reading, it was study, so it required some effort, it had to be regular and systematic. Being dyslexic, I have never found reading and writing easy, so without the encouragement of the community of Divine Innocence I would never have attempted the BA Divinity at Maryvale. Looking back, it had a seismic impact on my Faith. The Mass, all the Sacraments are more vibrant and prayer so much more lively. Together with the Eucharistic University, study has become a joy, because before Our Lord in the Blessed Sacrament the subject being studied leads into contemplation with deeper insights and understanding. I always found Adoration difficult, being very restless and with a limited attention span, but I have found Adoration combined with study at the Eucharistic University so much easier. It is not just Adoration, it is participation, a two-way relationship of teacher and student. (SM, England)

## Further Signs that God is Working through the Community

Members of the Community were asked about spiritual signs or miracles they had witnessed, because Our Lord had said in a message that the main miracle is the Way of Divine Innocence itself which will transform people's lives. Among the responses were:

- I still had not read the messages properly myself. Finally, one day, I did casually browse one and realised immediately that this was something extraordinary. However, the grace to embrace their content took longer. Over time I began to accept them, drawn to the truth in them and a desire to adopt what they were asking. (SM, England)
- I have seen some amazing graces received through the prayer of the Crucified Innocence Chaplet: unexpected reversal of trials within my family when this prayer was prayed with fervour and trust, broken relationships reversed and suffering in families healed. I use this prayer daily with trust and confidence in the outcomes. I honour Our Lady under the title: Mother of the Hidden and Mystical Wounds, wounds received at the foot of the Cross. She is our Mother and knows all our hidden wounds and desires our healing and conversion. What more powerful place could we be than at the foot of the Cross! (DW, England)
- By 1990 I had suffered with severe depression and gradually over those years my children went in all different directions (babies out of wedlock; alcohol; running away from home; anger and feeling totally

abandoned by God and their father). I understood what crucified innocence meant and I completely understood the need to come into the love and protection of the Holy Family within the Catholic Church. My journey back to the faith began when I stepped into the Novitiate of the Holy Family and made my commitment in 1991. Looking back, I see the incredible grace-filled journey and great healings my children and I have received over the years. They have all participated in the First Friday Walks of reparation. My eldest daughter has eight children and is a member too. I praise God they all married in the Catholic Church and my 15 grandchildren were baptised into the faith. (JL, Australia)

\*\*\*

What, in essence, do the members of the Community who are cited in these pages, including Patricia herself, the instrument of the inspiration, tell us by their witness? Their lives, by becoming more Christ-centred, were touched by the truth of the Divine Innocence messages. They learned that by recognising that they were members of the Holy Family they were able to appropriate the virtues of Jesus, Mary and St Joseph and follow their counsels, beyond simple imitation. By coming to more active praise of and gratitude to God and to love of others and being ready to witness to them, they began to live the grace that they received and consolidate their unity within the Holy Family. They prayed that Christ's Divine Innocence would be triumphant in their crucified innocence, and their prayers would bring blessings, not only on their own lives, but on their families, the Church, the world and other souls. The Community became more mature and showed greater understanding of the faith. The witness of the faith and lives of these and other members is the principal fruit of the Way of Divine Innocence to date, and it is by its fruit that the sound tree is known (cf. Matthew 7: 15-20).

Patricia summarises this witness as reflecting the life of the early Church:

*Patricia.* The first thing the Apostles did at the Resurrection was to witness to what they had seen and heard. They witnessed to the risen Christ. This inspiration witnesses to Christ's Divine Innocence, triumphant in all crucified innocence through his victory on the Cross, and to how we can participate fully in that victory through the Sacraments and teachings of the Catholic Church. (June 2017)

# Chapter Nine

---❈❈❈---

# The Claiming of the Victims of Abortion as Martyrs

A further remedy for the ills of the world proposed by Our Lord is that the Catholic Church should proclaim all children deliberately killed before birth as martyrs to the truths and teaching of the Church and recognise these children as companion martyrs of the Holy Innocents of Bethlehem. The cause of the new Holy Innocents is urgent because of the unprecedented shedding of innocent blood through abortion throughout the world. Abortion may no longer be a crime in most societies today, but in the eyes of the Catholic Church it disobeys the Fifth Commandment and is a serious sin against the Holy Spirit, '*the Lord, the giver of life*' (*Nicene Creed*). The killing of children by abortion and embryo experimentation constitutes a vast area of crucified innocence in these times. The children killed before birth are crucified in their innocence.

These children are therefore witnesses to Christ's victory over the sins that caused their deaths. He is victorious in them and triumphant in their crucified innocence. The Catholic Church is called to show forth Christ's victory in these millions of child-martyrs, so they can witness universally to the risen Christ in them and call those who have put them to death to the truth and to conversion. The Church, under the successor of Peter, is called to a great apostolic witness that will summon nations to the fullness of the Truth, to tell the world it has crucified Christ in these children. And when asked '*What shall we do now brethren?*' the Holy Father can but repeat St Peter's words: '*You must repent and be baptised every one of you, in the name of Jesus Christ, for the forgiveness of your sins.*' (Acts 2: 37-38)

Our Lord has given many references to Scripture, Tradition and the writings of the Fathers and the Saints, to Conciliar documents and to Papal teaching in support of this request. Because God created the children in his image and likeness, with immortal souls, he does not forget them. He raises them up through the power of Christ's passion and death, and his victory over sin and evil, won by his perfect sacrifice perpetuated in the Mass.

The messages show that the children are witnesses to the truth of the right to life that God has given them. They witness to Christ, who is '*the way, the truth and the life*'. (John 14:6) They are also witnesses to the truth of the teachings of the Catholic Church, the only universal motherly body which has the power, doctrine and teaching to claim the children as her own. It is the Church that has always upheld the children's right to life, considering the killing of these children as contrary to divine, natural and moral law.

By claiming these children for Christ, the Church will realise part of God's plan of salvation. In doing so, it will proclaim to the world, and particularly to their parents, that nothing is definitively lost. The parents are given the hope of being united with their child in the Communion of Saints in this world and hereafter. The children's short lives are enlightened by the promise of eternal life and renewed by the gift of divine life, which reaches its full realisation in eternity.[11]

For example, speaking of the children killed before birth and referring to Ezekiel, chapter 37, and the image of the dry bones, Jesus said to Patricia:

*Jesus.* Invoke the Spirit to breathe life into them in My Church! Then the whole world will see they are not the dry bones of sin and death strewn over a desert of sin and evil, but saints and martyrs who proclaim the truth and teachings of My Church. Let the Church study this chapter well. (4/12/1993)

*Patricia.* In the children, Our Lord found innocence crucified on a vast scale and he chose them to witness to his Divine Innocence triumphant over the sins and evil that had put them to death. The children were not guilty of actual sin, but only affected by original sin which

---

11  The Community of Divine Innocence has prepared a full documentation based on Scripture, Tradition and Church teaching that presents both evidence and a rationale for claiming the children by the Church. See the document, *Mercy Reigns*, available on the Divine Innocence website: www.divineinnocence.org.

was washed away in his blood. Claiming these children for Christ and his Church is the greatest act of mercy that the Church can carry out. (16/11/2016)

Commenting on Jeremiah 20:14-18, Jesus said:

*Jesus.*   Their mothers' womb is their tomb! But I too was imprisoned in a tomb, and the stone was rolled away, and I burst the bounds of the tomb. I am now asking the Church to roll away the stone that entombs[12] these souls and allow them to enjoy My Resurrection in the Church. It is now full time for them to awake from sleep and to be born from the womb of the Mother Church. (5/9/1995)

He has made repeated appeals for the Church to claim the victims of abortion as martyrs:

*Jesus.*   Let the Church claim and name these little martyred ones. Unprecedented evil calls for an unprecedented remedy and a mercy and grace that comes to the rescue of defenceless children. Do not turn these little ones away, for of such is the Kingdom of Heaven! (10/2/1992)

*Jesus.*   By the Church embracing these little ones

---

12   That entombs them in indifference, or in the belief that they do not exist, once killed.

and raising them before the world to their
martyr status, she proclaims My Saving Love
to all nations. She proclaims the Creed and
the teachings of the Church. She facilitates
their witness to Me, the Way, the Truth, and
the Life. I am the Prime Lover! This is a great
movement of My Love! I Am that I Am! Give
this message to the Church! (11/5/1999)

Jesus castigated abortion as a war-crime and a holocaust:

*Jesus.*    Is there a greater holocaust than scientists
and medical men using their God-given gifts
to experiment with the remains of murdered
human beings? They will be called to account
for taking part in these war-crimes. The
war against the helpless and the innocent is
of diabolical proportions... Scientists and
medical men and women would find the
cure for many problems if they would only
humble themselves and pray for the answer.
(7/10/1994)

And ten years later he renewed his request for the claiming
of the children as martyr witnesses by the authorities of the
Church:

*Jesus.*    The logic of Divine Love must tell you that
the little ones are in heaven. They are the new
Holy Innocents. Their cause is not yet met
by the authorities of My Church but met by

their God who saved them, washed away their original sin and raised them up to give Glory to their God, and to the Church, if she will but own them, glory to the children bathed in My Love, Mercy and Justice. They are Martyr Witnesses to the Truth that I Am, the Truth of the word disobeyed in their regard, the Truth of the right to life that I gave them. They enjoy life eternal in heaven where they wait to be recognised by their Mother, the Church. Their cause has been brought to the fore by the Mother of God, the Mother of the Hidden and Mystical Wounds. Their terrible wounds and crucifixion must no longer be hidden in the doubt, indifference, fear, and the disbelief of the hierarchy.

What have you got to lose? The claiming of these children and raising them to the Altar as companions of the first Holy Innocents will give glory to your God, glory to the Church, the children will be shown to be in glory, repentant sinners in their millions will be called to the Truth, a horrendous evil will be refuted, and mercy, love and justice will be proclaimed worldwide. This is what you will lose. (26/7/2009)

Patricia has several times sought the Lord's response to objections that have been made to recognising aborted children as martyrs.

*Patricia.* Lord, the aborted children did not actively consent to die for Christ or for the faith.

*Infant Jesus.* Nor did they actively deny the faith or Me. The first Holy Innocents did not actively consent to die for the faith or for Me – yet My Church says they died for Me and made them saints. (10/2/1992)

Summarising the great benefits that would accrue from the claiming, Patricia says:

*Patricia.* A priest made the comment that if the claiming took place all the rest would fall into place. It is the power the Church has available to her, in and through the Holy Spirit, by using the universal authority of the Pope, the successor of St Peter, and the Magisterium of the Catholic Church. The Holy Father and the Bishops need to exercise that power to defeat a great evil that is destroying millions made in God's image, and to allow these children to rise in the Church and strike fear into the forces of evil that have claimed the children's lives. The children are, so to speak, saints behind enemy lines, because they come from every country and are waiting to begin a powerful universal mission in and through the Church that will speak in every language worldwide. (9/1/2017)

\*\*\*

Members of the Community have taken up the cause of the children with great enthusiasm:

- We are unashamedly pro-life, but always with gentleness; never being judgmental about others. We know we all need God's mercy. We pray and do reparation for the sin of abortion and all sins against holy Innocence. (MS, England)
- Jesus' request that aborted children be claimed as companion martyrs to the Holy Innocents of Bethlehem gave me great joy. I felt like Simeon in the temple exclaiming 'My eyes have seen the salvation which you have prepared for all the nations to see' (Luke 2:30-31). (LG, England)

\*\*\*

Patricia's inspiration has been summarised in *Part Two* in terms that may be unfamiliar, but this is because it provides a greater light of the Holy Spirit on God's mercy. The principal prayer of the Community, '*O Divine Innocence, be triumphant in our crucified innocence*', contains the inspiration in its essence, a message of consolation, of truth and of love, by which we are brought into the Holy Family and into the presence of the Divine Innocence of Jesus. It is like the magical moment in the Christmas season when, in the crib, in the illustration of a Christmas card, at a carol concert, and above all at Midnight Mass, we glimpse first a possibility of personal intimacy with the Holy Family and then, as in the liturgies of Good Friday and the Easter Vigil, are confronted with the reality of the Cross and the whole Paschal mystery. Everything is thus encapsulated in this prayer. To understand it is to embrace the truth of both the divine Incarnation in the Holy Family and the hope of our redemption through the passion, death and Resurrection of Jesus Christ.

# PART THREE

*Divine Innocence In The Church And Society*

# Chapter Ten

---∞---

# The Way of Divine Innocence and the Church

## Approaches Made to the Church Authorities

Many attempts have been made to gain the interest and approval of Church authorities, theologians and clergy regarding the authenticity and significance of the Divine Innocence messages. There have been expressions of interest from some individual clergy, including several theologians, but officially there has so far only been a negative response, first from the local Archbishop and then from the Congregation for the Doctrine of the Faith (CDF).

Although Divine Innocence is a lay movement, it was not long before the activities of the group attracted the attention of several Catholic clergy. As the work became better known some prominent priests and theologians were in contact, and they began to study the messages of Divine Innocence and the theological grounds for the claiming of the children. A group of clergy organised a conference at Solesmes Abbey where a number of papers were presented giving consideration to the justification for claiming the victims of abortion as martyrs. Following the publication of the papers in *Abortion and Martyrdom*[13], Fr Aidan Nichols OP, who jointly chaired the consultation, sought to interest the Bishops of England and Wales but received little positive response.

*Patricia.* **The CDF statement, a very brief paper entitled** '*Observations and Concerns of the CDF on the writings of Mrs Patricia de Menezes and the Community of the Divine Innocence*'**, showed no reference to or knowledge of the detailed work that had been carried out by theologians who were of good standing in the Church. The statement also had a tone of ridicule which caused the Community distress as they had a deep concern for serious areas of need in the Church and society, including the training of families in a deeper and ongoing study of the Faith and Catholic Christian holiness, the sanctity of marriage, and the protection of, and reverence for, human life.**

---

13    See Fr Aidan Nichols OP (ed.), *Abortion and Martyrdom* (Leominster: Gracewing, 2002).

Since the issuing of the CDF statement, the Community has lost people, as the impression is given that it is doing something that is disobedient to the Church. Nothing could be further from the truth. People ask if the Way of Divine Innocence is condemned. We answer no, because we are not aware of any proper investigation. We were asked in Rome, has anyone come to interview the instrument or visit the Foundation? No one has done so. No one has ever come to speak to members of the Community or to find out what we are really about. (23/1/2017)

The main problem for the Church authorities, both the CDF and the local bishop in London, is that they assumed that 'Divine Innocence' refers to the Community and not to the person of Jesus, who is the manifestation of the Divine Innocence of the Blessed Trinity. So, they concluded that the Community itself is making a claim to be Divine Innocence. Close theological study of the writings sent to them, including the text of the prayers of the Community, and especially its central prayer, 'O Divine Innocence be triumphant in our crucified innocence' which is clearly addressed to God as Divine Innocence, would have avoided this error.

In what is presented as a further major objection, the CDF alleges that the Community claims to be 'the whole diamond'. This is a reference to the image of a diamond shown by Our Lord, but this is also misunderstood. It is Jesus who is the whole diamond.

*Jesus.*   The whole diamond of my Divine Innocence
has shone out ever more brilliantly over the
ages in the understanding of mankind....
There should be no fear or rivalry between the
orders and communities and the community
of My Divine Innocence – you will and must
be one! What diamond breaks itself up into
single facets? (19/1/2001)

*Patricia.* Our Lord was referring to an earlier
message that spoke of a great diamond
symbolising all facets of the Catholic faith:
the different orders, charisms, spiritualities
and movements within the Church. He
showed that Christ's Divine Innocence is the
whole diamond in its complete perfection.
(19/1/2001)

Furthermore, the CDF stated that the possibility of claiming
the victims of abortion as martyrs could not depend upon
a 'baptism of love' such as it asserted was being proposed.
However, the Community has never claimed that victims
of abortion simply receive a 'baptism of love'. Instead it is
affirmed that they have received a 'baptism of blood', like
that of the Holy Innocents. A baptism of love is mentioned
in the context that God loves these children and all
the Sacraments flow from the love of God and Christ's
Crucifixion, by which he died for the love of all mankind.
Our Lord stated that these children are not outside his
victory on the Cross over all sin and death including the
sins that brought about the death of these children. In its

response to the *Observations of the CDF*, the Community affirmed further of the aborted children: '*It is not only that they are a special category of innocent victim; it is Christ's saving choice of their witness to him, the Word, and to him as the source of grace upon whom they utterly depend.*'

The local Archbishop never answered these points which the Community sought to bring to his attention, but he none the less sought to restrict the Community's use of the name of Divine Innocence. Efforts to explore the matter further by letter have not found a response. It has been a disconcerting experience for the Community to be kept at a distance by the Church authorities. The Community argued that such a painful situation can only be resolved through dialogue. However, these misunderstandings have not so far been addressed or rectified, despite many appeals made for an opportunity to present the Community's case.

The Community has never been disobedient to the Church, but many members felt they could not continue until the Community was officially sanctioned by the hierarchy. The Community considered that something fundamentally important was at stake. They could not deny that Divine Innocence, whom they understood to be Christ himself, and the Way of his Divine Innocence have proved to be responsible for so many good things in their lives. Moreover, there has been no straying from the teaching of the Church, but only the encouragement to deepen the knowledge and practice of the Catholic Faith. The Community believes that the requests made, concerning both the establishment of the Community and the Novitiate of the Holy Family as a Catholic spirituality and the claiming of the children, have not yet been fully evaluated, and certainly not to the satisfaction of Jesus himself as he made clear in many further messages regarding the relevance and urgency of the requests being made to the Church.

How might the Church more fruitfully respond to the challenge posed by these messages? In the messages Patricia receives, there is an insistent voice that asks both for recognition of the Way of Divine Innocence and agreement to the claiming of the children killed by abortion as martyrs of the Church. Must the Church not look again at this comprehensive divine solution to such a serious plight facing mankind? Guidelines exist for how the Church should handle claims to private revelation. Surely there should be a right to be heard on the part of the recipient and a respectful dialogue between the recipient and the Church authorities?

It might be said that if Patricia had been able to say that what she is receiving are merely the fruits of prayer and meditation it would have been easier to obtain a dialogue; however she insists she cannot say that in good conscience.

*Patricia.* I was certainly not meditating or praying. I did not know Our Lady, and only knew Our Lord from a Protestant view. I was very suspicious and afraid of the Catholic Church and even of the Rosary, and when I came across Benediction one day in a church, I gathered up my children and left the church. I was afraid of what I thought was something displeasing to God and I was certainly not going to take part in it. I did not realise then that I was actually in the presence of Christ himself in the Blessed Sacrament. Our Lord and Our Blessed Lady gave me an amazing visual and instructional catechism. I was being taught the Catholic Faith and the joy of the truth was being opened up to me. This was not just for me; it was for the whole Church and the whole of the world. I was unable to deny the true origin of the inspiration. I feel that my witness is being stifled by the Church authorities. (23/1/2017)

## The Blessings the Inspiration Offers to the Church

What then are the potential benefits to the Church stemming from the Divine Innocence inspiration? They are many.

- There are the individual benefits for those who have committed themselves to the Way of Divine Innocence by striving to live as fitting members of the Holy Family.
- There are blessings for the Church from the teaching given by Jesus in the messages, and through the graces gained by those receiving a spiritual and practical training in the Way of Divine Innocence, in order to help them and their families lead lives of holiness.
- There is the benefit of a deeper recognition that all mankind, and especially the baptised, belong to the

original Order of the family founded by Jesus in the Holy Family as the Church in miniature.

- The Way of Divine Innocence, lived in the Order of the Holy Family, is the means to the renewal for those religious Orders in the Church that have been struggling to survive, and also for priests and religious who need constantly to renew and refine their charisms.
- There is the immense benefit to be derived from the claiming of the aborted children as martyrs and intercessors.
- There are blessings for the secular world from the correction that the Way of Divine Innocence brings to it, morally and spiritually.
- Many of the actual benefits have been shown in the witness statements in *Part Two* by people who made the commitment to the training within the Novitiate of the Holy Family in years past, and who testify to the value of this way of life, its prayers and its teachings under the care of Jesus, Mary and St Joseph.

In summary, what the Way of Divine Innocence shows is that it is in being guided by the Novitiate of the Holy Family that spiritual renewal will come about. It is an inspiration for the whole Church, clergy and lay faithful alike, that will help stimulate the new evangelisation in *ardour, method and expression* called for by Pope St John Paul II. Far from conflicting with other charisms, the Way of Divine Innocence would help all religious Orders in living their own charisms by increasing love and trust in Jesus, Mary and St Joseph. Lay people, by frequenting the Sacraments, praying for the protection and guidance of Jesus, Mary and St Joseph, interceding for the claiming of the children, studying the faith, and praying the Divine Office, would only do what they might otherwise have done, but now in union with the Holy Family and able to appropriate their virtues and receive tangible spiritual and practical help from them.

A divinely-inspired solution to the tragedy of abortion is being proposed: the model of the Holy Family, the motherly and fatherly roles of wife and husband, the protection of innocence, the claiming by the Catholic Church of aborted children as companion martyrs to the Holy Innocents, the recognition of God's mercy for those who repent of the sin of abortion, and the blessing of recognising its innocent victims as heavenly intercessors. The victims of abortion are the clearest example of crucified innocence in today's world. In this they share the fate of Jesus crucified and of all innocent victims of other people's sins. But Jesus is triumphant in their crucified innocence, since he came to save men by calling them to the Truth and showing them the way to salvation through the Church and by their participation in its saving life.

The earliest witnesses to the divine Order of the family are John the Baptist, who defended the sanctity of the marriage relationship in rebuking Herod, and the Holy Innocents, who witnessed by their blood to the sanctity of life. The claiming of the victims of abortion as martyrs, or witnesses, restores to the Holy Family of today's Church its most innocent members who were baptised in the blood of Christ and who are now in heaven, as Jesus has stated. The Holy Family, through the Novitiate, offers salvation to all families so that Divine Innocence can be triumphant in all areas of family life. Thus, the claiming of the children and the Novitiate of the Holy Family are mutually supportive elements of God's plan of salvation. It is now for the Church to give consideration and assistance to this plan of Heaven in our time, with all its apostolic authority.

# Chapter Eleven

---

# The Way of Divine Innocence and the Secular World

## The Spiritual Issues

In the years since this inspiration began, its timeliness and relevance have massively increased. The inspiration of Divine Innocence does not seek to alter the established teachings and pastoral practice of the Catholic Church, and certainly does not support bigotry or any condemnation of individuals who choose to live according to an alternative morality. Instead, it affirms the principle of divine mercy. However, there is a call to reject and refute those ideologies that call into question the perennial commitment of Catholic teaching to the place of marriage between man and woman as the bedrock of human community. It therefore opposes the changes that have occurred in the social and legislative status of marriage, the liberalisation of abortion, the growing acceptance of homosexual marriage and transgenderism, and the consequent confusion of the male and female genders created by God. These innovations have become icons of relativism in their denial of any truth or moral absolutes, and they are wholly incompatible with the divine Order of the Holy Family given to us by God for our safety and thriving.

The consequence of these developments has been to increase the state of vulnerability of the weakest in society by questioning the right to life, not only of the unborn but of the physically and mentally disabled, the sick, aged and those thought to be close to death. What further spiritual and psychological disorders can be expected for parents and societies that have made their accommodation to the culture of death by their radical undermining of the traditional family and their endorsement of a woman's 'right to choose' abortion without considering the rights of the child made in God's image?

The evident reality is that contemporary society, by ignoring God's divine Order, has become increasingly self-sufficient in its thinking. In the mistaken view that the most recent thinking is the best, customs, laws and behaviour are changing in extreme ways. Even in the Church there are those in responsible positions who endorse the taking of Holy Communion by those with multiple marriages and who give consent to gay unions, contraception and abortion. Orthodox Catholics everywhere are voicing the same protest: the unchangeable is being changed. Christianity is in increasing danger of appearing to be a social doctrine about rights, while often failing to affirm the most basic right of all, the right to life. We could yet see the true Church reduced to a remnant, as Pope Benedict warned, and that could entail social exclusion and even the criminalisation and persecution of those Christians who propose alternatives to the new, disordered moral consensus.

At a time when contemporary society is challenging fundamental tenets of Christianity in an unprecedented way, the Lord is shining a greater light on existing public revelation and the divine will. Mankind has deviated from his commandments and is changing the Order he founded. The breakdown of the family causes suffering in women and children first, then the role of men is degraded. Disorientation in their roles and disobedience to God's laws brings about all kinds of distress and huge financial costs to governments and individuals through sexual excesses, disease, mental health problems and social conflict. To confront this chaos, the divine Order is being proposed to us. We are being shown how to preserve that order in ourselves, our genders, our families, our societies and our nations. If we have moved away from God's divine Order, we are being offered the power of Christ's Divine Innocence to reclaim and preserve our innocence.

The first challenge to the secular world is therefore spiritual: "*The fool says in his heart, 'there is no God'.*" (Psalms 14 and 52) The abandonment by secular society of Christian-inspired values, especially those related to the family and to human life and sexuality, is virtually complete. The inspiration of Divine Innocence proposes a healing, a restoration of innocence and of the natural order inspired by the divine Order of the Holy Family. The greatest immediate challenge is over abortion and the proclaiming of the rights of the innocent unborn. These children have no voice. Heaven is asking the Catholic Church to give them a universal voice to witness to the Truth.

## The Claiming of Victims of Abortion

When Patricia was originally entrusted by Jesus with the Divine Innocence inspiration in the mid-1980s abortion was already a major moral issue for humanity. Indeed, in his apostolic letter *Humanae Vitae* (1968), Pope Paul VI had prophesied the consequences that would befall the world as a direct result of contraception: it would lead to promiscuity, the break-up of marriages and the increase of abortion. Although Church teaching on these issues has been very substantial at a theological level, particularly through Pope St John Paul's Apostolic Exhortation *Familiaris Consortio* (1981), his teaching on the theology of the body and the clear doctrine of the *Catechism of the Catholic Church*, the pastoral response of the Church in England has been very modest, apart from the valiant efforts of a few lay-led pro-life agencies. Over the past fifty years the calamities foretold by Pope Paul VI have occurred to a disastrous degree even within the community of the Church. The steady increase in abortion and the use of abortifacient contraception has seen the Church failing to respond with a sufficient degree of concerted moral leadership to have an impact on the lives even of Catholics.

As for secular society, it now sees abortion as a human right, and is fast moving towards regarding human life as a merely material good that can be surrendered or disposed of as soon as it appears burdensome to the victim or inconvenient to society at large. At the same time, secular powers have become enslaved to radical feminist and homosexualist ideologies. Along with a rise in divorce rates worldwide, and no less amongst Catholics, there has been the legal recognition of alternatives to the traditional family through the homosexualist revolution, and the gradual imposition of school curricula of sex education devoid of reference to morality, marriage or family life.

When the Church decides to claim the innocent victims of abortion as companion martyrs of the Holy Innocents, what will happen in a world convinced of the contention that abortion involves simply the mother's right to choose, regardless of the human and spiritual worth of the unborn child? Pro-life agencies inside and outside of the Church have battled courageously to publicise their condemnation of abortion and to argue for legal restrictions, but whatever their impact on public opinion, how far can they claim to have reversed public policies? Massive financing of contraceptive and abortion agencies continues unchecked in the western world and is increasingly associated with pressures on third-world countries to expand human 'reproductive rights' and facilities, commonly understood as involving access to abortion.

There are forces that want to make sure that the untold millions of children killed before birth are never claimed by the Catholic Church as witnesses to the Truth that comes from God and which is taught by the Church. They desire at all costs to stop the children's Christian witness reaching their parents, legislators, governments, and the clinical agencies who make money from the killing of these children. These forces of evil take no account of the fact that many mothers and fathers will never forget they were involved in the death of their own innocent children. Those that have claimed the children's lives can well marvel at the power and beauty of this message of mercy, forgiveness and love. Once the Catholic Church claims the children for Christ and his Church, a mighty army of Holy Innocents will arise in the Church, and people will know they can pray to them as saints and find reconciliation. Our Lord gave the children the name *'Mercy Reigns'* because he wants all to receive his mercy and forgiveness and strive to reach heaven to be with God and his saints for all eternity.

The restoration of a culture of life and love cannot merely consist in a re-affirmation of the doctrine of traditional marriage, even though this lies at the core of its spirituality. The commitment to ending abortion is a major practical development of the Way of Divine Innocence, rather than a separate element of its implications for society. The fate of the unborn cannot be separated from the wholesome view of sexuality espoused by the teaching of the Way of Divine Innocence. The family was instituted for love and for the transmission of life through love. Any barrier to this process is in wanton disregard for God's will. Secular society thus stands challenged by the Way of Divine Innocence, and indeed by the whole beauty and good sense of Catholic moral teaching, for its compromise with the culture of death along with its erroneous ideologies affirming women's 'right to choose' abortion, gender confusion and abandonment of God-given rules for authentic love between the two sexes.

# Chapter Twelve

---

# An Act of Trust in God's Will

Patricia does not claim to have foreknowledge of what will transpire regarding the inspiration of Divine Innocence, except that she is assured that the message will eventually be heard and that the claiming of the children will occur. Her role is to trust in God and continue to seek to make his messages known, and to live by them. Equally, it is hoped that this present writing will encourage interest and devotion among the people of God and hasten the day when the Church will approve the good practical and moral sense of this private revelation and give effect to the proposals it contains.

The Community of Divine Innocence seeks acceptance by the Catholic Church authorities. In so doing it places its trust in the divine will which the community believes desires this outcome. In this sense, the mission of the Way of Divine Innocence is seen as a prophetic work which will achieve what Our Lord wishes. There is to be a church near the Foundation House. It will be the first church dedicated to the Lord's Divine and Crucified Innocence and will be a place of pilgrimage. The Community of Divine Innocence is called to teach and diffuse a spirituality based on the life of the Holy Family of Nazareth as a means of sanctification appropriate to the times and destined for all.

It is remarkable to note that, on the Feast of the Beatified Martyrs of England and Wales in 1985, Our Lady called the Divine Innocence inspiration a great grace to England through their supplication. She followed this several weeks later with the message:

> **O England! Come back into the arms of your Mother! Let me, the Immaculate Mother of God, heal the wounds of disunity and disobedience.** (23/7/1985)

And two years later:

> **England, my dowry. How this little title protects you, and what a grace it has brought you – God's acknowledgement of your great martyrs and saints, and still more to come in this new age of Divine Innocence! O England, how I love you!...** **In you, England, has been born the Message of Triumphant Crucified Innocence.** (3/7/1987)

Our Lady appeals to the Church in England to be faithful to the great tradition and zeal of its martyrs whose prayers for their country are now being answered, no doubt including those for the cause of the martyrs in the womb.

Secular society has no impulse to reverse its stance on abortion without the Church, but if the Church proclaims the martyr status of children killed before birth by abortion this will surely have a transformative effect. It will provide a prophetic witness to the nations that cannot be silenced. These children's martyr witness can speak in every language, in every place where abortion is practised. In their death, Christ is crucified anew in them; they become Christ's Crucified Innocence. Like him they are innocent victims of other people's sins. Their witness can, through the Church, proclaim God's justice, mercy and love to millions of people who have contributed to their deaths.

It is not enough to say that the Lord has already won the battle for the unborn and that we are to wait in trust for the disappearance of abortion. The claiming of the children by the Catholic Church effectively opens a way to call all those involved in the children's deaths to repent and believe in the Gospel of life. The moral and spiritual challenge provoked will strike deep into the culture, evangelising it and helping restore a culture of life and love in place of the currently prevailing culture of death.

Reflection on the theology of Divine Innocence reveals the link between the Way of Divine Innocence and the claiming of the children. The central relevance of the Holy Family to Christian spirituality implies a definitive solution to the issue of abortion. It is impossible to continue to hold in tension the exemplary status of the Holy Family and the wantonness of society's attitude to the unborn as wholly without rights. Jesus became God Incarnate at his conception. Every child is analogously gifted with not only human but spiritual life from its very beginning. One is inconceivable without the other. This argument should be very clear to the Church, and must eventually lead to the claiming of the children. For how much longer can the assertion of human rights without acceptance of the rights of the unborn continue to convince, or to deceive?

This inspiration simply proclaims the good news of salvation that comes through the incarnation of Divine Innocence and our becoming more like the Christ-child. It also provides a practical step towards countering the secular justification for abortion as a choice for mothers, by affirming the family as modelled on the Holy Family of Nazareth with its expression of the love and unity of man and wife in the care and nurturing of the children that God grants. The faithful are invited to live in union with the Holy Family, to study their faith diligently, and to intercede as prayer warriors for an end to abortion through the claiming of the children.

The teaching of Divine Innocence is sound, logical, salvific and fully Catholic. The Church, which is obliged by the Gospel and papal teaching to help form a civilisation of love, needs to hear this message clearly and plainly. The issue is in God's hands and, if this inspiration is of God, it will not be repudiated.

We can no doubt trust that, in his own time, Jesus will win over the hearts of the Church authorities to the recognition of the apostolic power of the Novitiate of the Holy Family and the cause of the claiming. My own earlier book, *Heaven Wants to be Heard,* was a study of the convergences to be found in the messages from several cases of private revelation that are in the majority being held at arm's length by the Church, even though up to now none has been condemned. The caution of the Church is in one sense admirable, since the faithful need to be protected from doctrinal error, but the evidence is that, in this instance, Heaven does want to be heard. Millions of mothers and fathers of these children need to hear their own children's witness to the Truth and that they are alive in heaven, triumphant in Christ's Divine Innocence. Governments, legislators and those in the medical profession who have had a hand in the death of these children need the truth to be proclaimed.

Therefore, the Church has the responsibility to discern definitively, and not to delay her active response and decisions, leaving this charism to suffer a trial by neglect. The Church is withholding a great consolation from mothers and fathers as well as a universal correction to those who condone abortion. Is it right to delay God's touching the hearts of millions of people? Our Lord has asked how many more feasts of All Saints will go by without the adding of this vast array of martyrs to those included in the feast-day celebrations whose intercession people can seek?

Undoubtedly the principal aim of the Lord's interventions is that of restoring the supernatural to general consciousness in secular society, and especially in the whole area of the sacredness of human life as God's gift to each individual person and to the world.

*Jesus.* My children, you see how important it is for the Way of My Divine Innocence to spread everywhere. I wish to reclaim the wasteland of sin and to give My children the innocence that is their inheritance, so together we can have joy. I wish to transform families, young people, priests, governments, workplaces (the whole of society). I wish to renew the face of the earth and see Holy Innocence blossom everywhere. It is because you have believed that this is possible that I have come to each one of you to ask you to co-operate in this longing desire of my Heart. I need your suffering, offered generously for souls. (20/7/1997)

\*\*\*

The essential role of the Community is to disseminate the Divine Innocence messages of hope, in order to help bring about conversion and healing from the moral disasters that are being perpetrated in society. Our Lord says that it is by living the Way of Divine Innocence that we will see change, but this living must be by word and deed. This is what will evangelise not only the Church's members but all of society and, with the help of grace, make the Divine Innocence of Christ triumphant in our crucified innocence. It is the Way of Divine Innocence that provides the solution to the crisis of the family, and that will restore its holiness and protect life, including the life of the unborn, through the intercession, training and guidance of the Holy Family in the living Novitiate of the foundational Order created by God. The message of Divine Innocence is that of the Gospel, or as Jesus said, '*a greater light of the Holy Spirit on public revelation*' (7/4/1997), and a missionary action proposed to the Church and to human society in our time.

For any further information about The Family of Divine Innocence, please contact:

The Family of Divine Innocence
PO Box 676A, Surbiton,
Surrey KT5 8WR,
United Kingdom

or visit:

www.divineinnocence.org

or request information by email from: enquiry@divineinnocence.org